CASUAL DAY HAS GONE TOO FAR

A DILBERT® BOOK BY SCOTT ADAMS

First published in 1997 by Andrews and McMeel, a Universal Press Syndicate Company,
4520 Main Street, Kansas City, Missouri 64111, USA

This edition published in 1997 by Boxtree, an imprint of Macmillan Publishers Ltd,
25 Eccleston Place, London, SW1W 9NF and Basingstoke

Associated companies throughout the world

ISBN 0 7522 1119 6

Copyright © 1997 United Feature Syndicate, Inc.

All rights reserved. No part of this publication may be reproduced, stored in or introduced into a retrieval system, or transmitted, in any form, or by any means (electronic, mechanical, photocopying, recording or otherwise) without the prior written permission of the publisher. Any person who does any unauthorized act in relation to this publication may be liable to criminal prosecution and civil claims for damage.

DILBERT® is a registered trademark of United Feature Syndicate, Inc.

DILBERT and DOGBERT appear in the comic strip DILBERT®, distributed by
United Feature Syndicate, Inc.

http://www.unitedmedia.com/comics/dilbert

9 8 7 6 5 4 3 2 1

A CIP catalogue record for this book is available from the British Library

Printed and bound in Great Britain by Mackays of Chatham PLC, Kent

This book is sold subject to the condition that it shall not, by way of trade or otherwise, be lent, re-sold, hired out, or otherwise circulated without the publisher's prior consent in any form of binding or cover other than that in which it is published and without a similar condition including this condition being imposed on the subsequent purchaser.

For

Pam "Why-Do-You-Sneeze-When-I-Talk?" Okasaki

Other Dilbert Books from Boxtree

Shave The Whales

ISBN: 0 7522 0849 7

Bring Me The Head of Willy The Mailboy!

ISBN: 0 7522 0136 0

Always Postpone Meetings With Time-Wasting Morons

ISBN: 0 7522 0854 3

Still Pumped From Using The Mouse

ISBN: 0 7522 2265 1

Access Denied – Dilbert's Quest For Love in the Nineties

ISBN: 0 7522 2421 2

Telling It Like It Isn't

ISBN: 0 7522 2426 3

It's Obvious You Won't Survive By Your Wits Alone

ISBN: 0 7522 0201 4

The Dilbert Principle

ISBN: 0 7522 2287 2 (hardback edition)
ISBN: 0 7522 2470 0 (paperback edition)

The Dilbert Future

ISBN: 0 7522 1118 8

Dogbert's Top Secret Management Handbook

ISBN: 0 7522 2410 7

Introduction

I was in the bookstore the other day, hiding in the back reading a new car buying guide, and suddenly I felt very ripped-off. I realized the book had no introduction!

This shortcoming was not mentioned anywhere on the cover of the book. In fact, I had almost finished getting all the information I needed before I even realized the introduction was missing. I felt violated. Used. Dirty.

I stomped over to the cash register, pausing only long enough to de-alphabetize some of the books in the kids section. (I do that because the children are our future, which can't possibly be a good thing, so I try to slow them down when I can.)

I waited patiently in line—to demonstrate that I am a reasonable man—then I demanded my money back. Predictably, the bookstore employee started spouting a bunch of "rules" they have about refunds. I discovered they are totally inflexible about the fact that the customer must buy the book before a refund can be issued. I argued that my ownership of the book was clearly established by all the yellow highlighting I had done. This logic fell on deaf ears.

I took a deep breath to gather my composure, muttered something unintelligible about "repeat business" and stormed over to the magazine section to catch up on my reading.

Frankly, I don't know how the bookstore stays in business with service like that.

But this ugly episode got me thinking about the value of book introductions. I realized that I have an obligation as an author to do more than just take your money. I also have an obligation to fill up a certain number of pages.

And speaking of obligations, there's still time to join Dogbert's New Ruling Class (DNRC) and get the free Dilbert newsletter too. As you've probably heard, when Dogbert conquers the world, the DNRC will form his elite inner circle. Everyone else, the so-called induhviduals, will be available as our domestic servants.

The Dilbert newsletter is free and it's published approximately "whenever I feel like it," which is about four times a year. There's an e-mail version and a snail mail version. The e-mail version is better.

E-mail subscription (preferred): write to scottadams@aol.com

Snail mail:

Dilbert Mailing List
c/o United Media
200 Madison Avenue
New York, NY 10016

S. Adams

http://www.unitedmedia.com/comics/dilbert

DOGBERT EXPLAINS LEADERSHIP
LEADERS START THEIR CAREERS AS MORONS.
S. Adams
THEY ARE DRAWN TO MEETINGS LIKE MOTHS TO A PORCH LIGHT.
THE SUCCESSFUL MORON WILL HAVE A VERY HIGH BLADDER-TO-BRAIN RATIO.
BRAIN
BLADDER
THEY PREVAIL IN ALL DECISIONS BECAUSE THEY ARE IMPERVIOUS TO LOGIC OR COFFEE.
LET'S DO IT MY WAY!
OKAY!
© 1995 United Feature Syndicate, Inc.
THESE QUALITIES ARE PERCEIVED AS LEADERSHIP.
YOU'RE PROMOTED!
2-5
AFTER SEVERAL PROMOTIONS THEIR JOB TENDS TO MATCH THEIR TALENTS.
I AWARD YOU THIS AWARD.
CONCLUSION: LEADERSHIP IS NATURE'S WAY OF REMOVING MORONS FROM THE PRODUCTIVE FLOW.

I'M PUTTING YOU ON THE STRATEGIC PLANNING TEAM.
S. Adams
IT'S LIKE WORK BUT WITHOUT THE SATISFACTION OF ACCOMPLISHING ANYTHING.
YOU'RE NEW, SO LET ME EXPLAIN HOW THIS WORKS.
WE HAVE MEETINGS AND TALK ABOUT THE COMPANY'S STRATEGY IN VAGUE EMOTIONAL TERMS.
IN TIME, WE CONVINCE OURSELVES THAT WE'RE MORE THAN MEDIOCRE THINKERS WHO SIT AROUND COMPLAINING.
2-12
© 1995 United Feature Syndicate, Inc.
WE START BELIEVING OUR OPINIONS WILL STEER THE COMPANY. WE FEEL IMPORTANT. WE FEEL **ALIVE**!!
THEN WE SNAP OUT OF IT AND MAKE VIEWGRAPHS THAT SAY WE SHOULD KEEP DOING WHAT WE'RE DOING.
I LIKE MAKING VIEW-GRAPHS.
ACTUALLY, WE USE LAST YEAR'S VIEWGRAPH.

I'M ASKING EVERYBODY TO QUANTIFY THEIR CONTRIBUTIONS TO REVENUE. YOUR PAY WILL DEPEND ON IT.
2/13
S. Adams
I REALIZE THIS IS HARD TO QUANTIFY BECAUSE YOU'RE DESIGNING FUTURE PRODUCTS BUT...
HERE YOU GO.
© 1995 United Feature Syndicate, Inc. (NYC)
A BILLION DOLLARS? IT'S AS IF YOU CYNICALLY BELIEVE WE CAN'T TRACK THESE NUMBERS.
THAT CROSSED MY MIND.
YOU SHOULD ALL FOLLOW WALLY'S EXAMPLE OF HOW HE QUANTIFIES HIS CONTRIBUTION TO REVENUE.
S. Adams
BASICALLY, I ASSUMED MY PROJECT WOULD FAIL WITHOUT ME. THEREFORE ALL THE REVENUE IT GENERATES CAN BE ATTRIBUTED TO ME.
2/14 © 1995 United Feature Syndicate, Inc. (NYC)
AREN'T WE ALL ON THE SAME PROJECT?
YES, BUT EVIDENTLY WE'RE NOT ALL EQUALLY VALUABLE.

WALLY, YOU JUST SENT ME THE SAME E-MAIL YOU SENT LAST WEEK.
S. Adams
I'M RERUNNING THE "BEST OF WALLY" WHILE I'M ON IN-CUBE SABBATICAL.
2/15 © 1995 United Feature Syndicate, Inc. (NYC)
HOW LONG IS YOUR SABBATICAL?
SIX MONTHS SO FAR, AND YOU'RE THE FIRST TO NOTICE.

I WAS SO LATE I HAD TO PUT ON MY MAKEUP IN THE CAR.
YEAH, I HAD TO SHAVE IN THE CAR.
THAT'S NOTHING. I WAS SO LATE THAT I HAD TO GIVE MYSELF A SPONGE BATH IN THE CAR.
AREN'T YOU THE DRIVER FOR YOUR CARPOOL?
YOU'VE NEVER HEARD SUCH WHINING.

THE PROBLEM...
WE'RE SO UNDER-STAFFED THAT THE PROJECT IS SIX WEEKS BEHIND SCHEDULE.
THE ANALYSIS...
I CAN'T ADD PEOPLE... I CAN'T CHANGE THE DUE DATE... I CAN'T IGNORE IT.
THE RESULT...
HE WANTS DAILY STATUS REPORTS UNTIL THE SITUATION IMPROVES.

BAD NEWS
WE'RE NOT GIVING ANY RAISES.
MAKING IT WORSE
BUT WE THINK WORK IS ITS OWN REWARD.
MAKING IT MUCH WORSE
EXPECT TO GET REWARDED ABOUT TWICE AS MUCH NEXT YEAR.

BOSS TYPES
FIND YOUR BOSS ON THIS HANDY REFERENCE.
S. ADAMS
HOSTAGE TAKER: TRAPS YOU IN YOUR CUBICLE AND TALKS YOUR EARS OFF.
BLAH BLAH
OW!!
FRAUD: USES VIGOROUS HEAD-NODDING TO SIMULATE COMPREHENSION.
THEN WE'LL SUBNET OUR I.P. ADDRESSES.
OH YEAH OH YEAH
MOTIVATIONAL LIAR: HAS NO CLUE WHAT YOU DO BUT SAYS YOU'RE THE BEST.
NOBODY CAN DO WHAT YOU DO!!
EXCEPT A MUSHROOM.
OVER PROMOTED: TRIES TO MASK INCOMPETENCE WITH POOR COMMUNICATION.
LET'S QUALITIZE OUR PARADIGM SO WE DON'T OVER INUNDATE WITH DATUMS.
© 1995 United Feature Syndicate, Inc.
WEASEL: TAKES CREDIT FOR YOUR HARD WORK.
THIS BONUS IS FOR BRILLIANTLY FORCING YOUR STAFF TO WORK 80 HOUR WEEKS.
IT WASN'T EASY!
$
2-19
MOSES: PERPETUALLY WAITS FOR CLEAR SIGNALS FROM ABOVE.
DON'T DO ANYTHING IMPORTANT YET.
NEVER HAVE.
PERFECT BOSS: DIES OF NATURAL CAUSES ON A THURSDAY AFTERNOON.
SHOULD WE DO SOMETHING?
THREE DAY WEEKEND!

RELIABLE SOURCES SAY YOUR PROJECT WILL BE CANCELLED, DILBERT.
2/20
YOU SHOULD ABANDON IT NOW AND COME WORK ON MY PROJECT. WHEN MY BIG PROMOTION GOES THROUGH NEXT MONTH, I'LL TRANSFER YOU TO MY GROUP AND GIVE YOU A RAISE.
S. Adams
© 1995 United Feature Syndicate, Inc.
THAT'S VERY TEMPTING EXCEPT FOR THE FACT YOU'RE A PATHOLOGICAL LIAR.
BE CAREFUL WHAT YOU SAY - I HAVE SUPER POWERS.
DOGBERT, I NEED YOUR HELP DEALING WITH A PATHOLOGICAL LIAR AT WORK.
2/21
YOU'RE IN LUCK. I HAPPEN TO HAVE A PH.D. IN LIATOLOGY FROM THE MASSACHUSETTS INSTITUTE OF TECHNOLOGY.
S. Adams
© 1995 United Feature Syndicate, Inc. (NYC)
I'D LOVE TO SEE YOUR DIPLOMA.
I'LL MAIL IT TO YOU.

WE'VE BEEN HAVING A PROBLEM WITH BLACK-OUTS. THE OFFICE LIGHTS ARE CONTROLLED BY MOTION DETECTORS.
S. Adams
I HIRED A TEMP TO WALK AROUND AND FLAP HIS ARMS SO THE LIGHTS WON'T GO OFF.
2/22 © 1995 United Feature Syndicate, Inc. (NYC)
ANOTHER JOURNALISM MAJOR ENTERS THE WORKFORCE.
IT SEEMS LIKE A WASTE. MAYBE HE COULD FAN US.

ALICE, I'M ALMOST DONE WITH YOUR PERFORMANCE APPRAISAL.
GASP
S. Adams
I HAVEN'T HAD AN APPRAISAL IN FOUR YEARS. YOU MUST BE STARTING A DOCUMENTATION TRAIL SO YOU CAN FIRE ME LATER.
2/23
© 1995 United Feature Syndicate, Inc. (NYC)
I'LL WORK 24 HOURS A DAY!!
THAT WAS WAY MORE MOTIVATIONAL THAN I'D HOPED.

I'M TERRIFIED ABOUT MY PERFORMANCE REVIEW TOMORROW.
2/24
S. Adams
MEN HAVE IT EASIER. YOU'VE BEEN CONDITIONED BY YEARS OF REJECTION AND GENERAL DISDAIN.
WE'RE LUCKY THAT WAY.
© 1995 United Feature Syndicate, Inc. (NYC)
OVERALL, I RATED YOUR PERFORMANCE AS "SIMIAN."
THANKS!

I'VE REPLACED THE OLD RATING SYSTEM WITH A FRIENDLIER METHOD. NOW I COMPARE EACH OF YOU TO AN ANIMAL WITH SIMILAR TRAITS.
S. Adams
I RATED YOU "TYRANNOSAURUS REX."
2/25
© 1995 United Feature Syndicate, Inc. (NYC)
T. REX – THE MIGHTIEST DINOSAUR!!
THINK IN TERMS OF BRAIN SIZE.

HERE'S SOME NICE CHOCOLATE CAKE FOR YOU AND DOGBERT.
THANKS, MOM.
THANKS, MOM.
S.Adams
TELL ME ALL ABOUT YOUR JOB AT THE RAILROAD.
IT'S NOT A RAILROAD. I'M AN ENGINEER AT A BIG CORPORATION.
DO YOU FIX THE TYPEWRITERS WHEN THEY BREAK?
NO... TODAY I DEBUGGED A TCP/IP DRIVER FOR AN APPLICATION THAT RUNS OVER ISDN WITH BONDING.
© 1995 United Feature Syndicate, Inc.
YOU MEAN, ALL YOU DO IS SLAP A BRI ANALYZER ON A CIRCUIT AND LOOK FOR BAD PACKETS?
2-26
WELL... YEAH.
BUT IT'S REALLY HARD.
I WAS DOING OKAY UNTIL SHE OFFERED TO PAY MY TUITION TO TYPEWRITER REPAIR SCHOOL.
YOU SHOULDN'T HAVE COMPARED HER CAKE TO PACKING FOAM.

I'M HAPPY TO REPORT THAT THE "EXCELLENCE IN TEAMING" READ-OUT IS NEARLY READY.
S. Adams
IT'S TAKEN FORTY PEOPLE FROM A DOZEN DEPARTMENTS TO COMPLETE THE STUDY. WE FINALLY GOT COMPLETE BUY-IN.
© 1995 United Feature Syndicate, Inc. (NYC)
IS THAT THE STUDY OF WHY WE CAN'T MAKE DECISIONS?
ORIGINALLY. BUT IT EVOLVED INTO MORE OF A DISCUSSION OF SQUIRREL MIGRATION PATTERNS.
2/27

AND TED GETS THIS "SINGULAR ACHIEVEMENT" AWARD FOR CREATING THE "WE ARE TEAMS" CAMPAIGN.
S. Adams
IT'S A CHECK FOR A THOUSAND DOLLARS! LET'S ALL GIVE TED A HAND.
© 1995 United Feature Syndicate, Inc. (NYC)
SLAP
WHACK
OW!!
THESE THINGS NEVER WORK THE WAY YOU WANT THEM TO.
2/28

WHY IS IT THAT I NEVER HAVE TIME TO EAT BUT YOU MEN ARE IN HERE EVERY DAY AT 11:35?
3/1
S. Adams
BECAUSE THE HOURS WE SPENT UPGRADING OUR PCs HAVE FINALLY PAID OFF BY GREATLY IMPROVING OUR EFFICIENCY.
© 1995 United Feature Syndicate, Inc. (NYC)
I THOUGHT IT WAS BECAUSE WE GET HUNGRY AT 11:30.
WE CAN'T REVEAL ALL OUR SECRETS.

WE'RE ANNOUNCING TWO NEW PROGRAMS FOR EMPLOYEES.
S. Adams
THE FIRST IS A NEW DIGNITY ENHANCEMENT PROGRAM AND THE SECOND IS OUR NEW RANDOM DRUG TESTING INITIATIVE.
3/2 © 1995 United Feature Syndicate, Inc. (NYC)
THE CLUE METER IS READING ZERO.
YOU EACH GET A HANDSOME COFFEE MUG AS PART OF THE KICK-OFF.
DROP YOUR TROUSERS AND TURN AROUND. I NEED A DNA SAMPLE.
3/3
S. Adams
WE'RE SCANNING FOR ANY FATAL GENETIC PROBLEMS THAT COULD HURT PRODUCTIVITY.
© 1995 United Feature Syndicate, Inc. (NYC)
UH... WE DECIDED TO MOVE YOUR PROJECT DEADLINE UP A WEEK.
FROM NOW ON, SALARIES WILL BE BASED ON YOUR PREDICTED SUCCESS, NOT YOUR PAST PERFORMANCE.
3/4
S. Adams
WE RAN A COMPUTER MODEL AGAINST YOUR EDUCATION AND DNA INFORMATION. WE PREDICT YOU'LL DIE
IN A STAPLER MISHAP WITHIN A WEEK.
© 1995 United Feature Syndicate, Inc. (NYC)
WHAT IF I DISAGREE WITH THIS PREDICTION?
WRITE UP YOUR OPINION AND STAPLE IT TO THE ANALYSIS.

WE'RE GOING DOWNTOWN TO PLAY "SECURITY GUARDS IN SPACE."
I DON'T WANT TO KNOW.
GEEK WEEK
S. Adams
LET'S TRY THAT BUILDING.
LUNCH
I'LL NEED TO SEE YOUR I.D. BADGE, SIR.
LOOK FAST!! THERE IT IS!! NOT A PACK OF MATCHES!!
OKAY
ZIP!
I'LL HAVE TO SEARCH YOUR LUNCH BOX.
© 1995 United Feature Syndicate, Inc.
IT'S JUST A BUNCH OF WIRES AND GIZMOS.
YOU'RE MAKING ME SO HUNGRY.
LUNCH
COULD YOU WATCH MY LUNCH WHILE I TAKE THE CART BACK TO MY CAR?
3-5
I FEEL BAD, BUT IT'S THE ONLY WAY TO TEST IF SPACE TRAVEL IS SAFE FOR US ANIMALS.
I FEEL SAFER ALREADY.

CAN YOU EXPLAIN WHY YOU'RE A WEEK BEHIND SCHEDULE?
S. Adams
YOUR POOR LEADERSHIP HAS DRAINED ME OF THE ENTHUSIASM THAT IS NECESSARY TO SUCCEED. BUT IT'S NOT COMPLETELY YOUR FAULT.
3-6
© 1995 United Feature Syndicate, Inc. (NYC)
FRANKLY, YOUR PARENTS HAVE TO ACCEPT SOME RESPONSIBILITY FOR CREATING YOU.
EVEN IF THEY WERE DRUNK?

WE NEED TO FINISH YOUR PROGRAM TWICE AS FAST, SO I'M ADDING A PERSON TO HELP YOU.
S. Adams
YOU MIGHT NEED TO TRAIN HIM A LITTLE BEFORE HE'S PRODUCTIVE.
WARNING! WARNING! DR. SMITH
3-7 © 1995 United Feature Syndicate, Inc. (NYC)
TELL ME AGAIN WHAT THE BIG GLOWING THING IS.

ARE YOU WORKING TWICE AS FAST SINCE I DOUBLED YOUR STAFF?
S. Adams
I'VE CODED TWELVE MODULES... BARRY IS ON A JOURNEY OF DISCOVERY WHERE HE WILL FIND OUT MY MOUSE IS NOT A MICROPHONE.
HELLO! ANYBODY!
3-8 © 1995 United Feature Syndicate, Inc. (NYC)
THAT WOULD EXPLAIN WHY NOBODY EVER COMMENTS ON MY ANNOUNCEMENTS OVER THE P.A. SYSTEM.

FROM NOW ON, THE MANAGERS AT MY LEVEL WILL BE CALLED "THOUGHT LEADERS."
WHAT'S WRONG WITH THIS PICTURE?
S. Adams
3-9 © 1995 United Feature Syndicate, Inc. (NYC)

YOUR PERFORMANCE THIS YEAR WAS GOOD, BUT YOU WORKED ON TASKS THAT AREN'T IMPORTANT. THEREFORE YOU GET A TINY RAISE.
I WORKED ON THE TASKS YOU ASSIGNED. WHAT'S THAT SAY ABOUT YOUR PERFORM-ANCE?
IT'S EXCELLENT. I GET A BONUS FOR KEEPING SALARIES LOW.
HAVE YOU SEEN ANY LITERATURE ON WORKPLACE VIOLENCE?
S. Adams
3-10 © 1995 United Feature Syndicate, Inc. (NYC)

UH-OH... THE MANAGERS ARE GOING TO ANOTHER CLOSED-DOOR MEETING.
IT MUST BE ABOUT PAY CUTS OR LAYOFFS. I'M DOOMED. I'D BETTER WORK ON MY RÉSUMÉ NOW.
OKAY, SO FAR OUR "LEADERSHIP VISION" SAYS "WE INSPIRE EMPLOYEES TO ACTION." DOES ANYBODY HAVE UPGRADES?
NAH
S. Adams
3-11 © 1995 United Feature Syndicate, Inc. (NYC)

DID YOU REVIEW MY DRAFT DOCUMENTATION YET?
UH... I'LL GET TO IT SOON.
S. Adams
THAT'S WHAT YOU'VE BEEN SAYING SINCE JULY!!
I KNOW I'M ONLY A LOWLY TECHNICAL WRITER AND YOU'RE A BIG IMPORTANT ENGINEER...
BUT IS IT TOO MUCH TO ASK FOR YOU TO GLANCE AT THE FRUITS OF MY LABORS?!!!
FIVE LOUSY MINUTES IS ALL IT WOULD TAKE TO VALIDATE MY VALUE ON THIS PLANET! READ IT, YOU FETID PILE OF COMPOST!!
© 1995 United Feature Syndicate, Inc.
OKAY, OKAY! I'LL READ IT RIGHT NOW!
THESE PAGES ARE BLANK! YOU'VE BEEN BLUFFING FOR MONTHS!
3-12
I THINK I'LL GO HAVE A YUMMY COMPOST SALAD WITH DELICIOUS FETID CHEESE.
I'M GOING TO LOOK UP THOSE WORDS.

I PROMISE THAT IF I DECIDE TO BUY YOUR COMPANY I'LL GLADLY RECOMMEND A POSITION FOR EACH OF YOU.
REALLY? YOU'D MAKE SURE WE ALL GOT JOBS?
S. Adams
3-13 © 1995 United Feature Syndicate, Inc. (NYC)
NO, BUT I'LL RECOMMEND A "POSITION."

MY CONSULTANT WILL AUDIT YOUR COMPANY TO MAKE SURE THERE ARE NO SURPRISES BEFORE I BUY IT.
I USE HIM BECAUSE HE'S SEEN SUCH HIDEOUS THINGS THAT NOTHING SCARES HIM.
ERK
S. Adams
3-14 © 1995 United Feature Syndicate, Inc. (NYC)
AAAAAEEII!!
OOOUWAA
WAA!!
THAT'S NOT THE SOUND YOU WANT FROM YOUR AUDITOR.

YOUR STOCK WAS $30 PER SHARE WHEN I OFFERED TO BUY THE COMPANY, BUT THANKS TO SOME TIMELY LEAKS TO THE MEDIA YOUR VALUE HAS PLUNGED.
HOWEVER, IF YOU SELL RIGHT NOW I'LL PAY THE FULL $30 FOR YOUR STOCK.
I RECOMMEND WE DO IT.
S. Adams
3-15 © 1995 United Feature Syndicate, Inc. (NYC)
DONE. $30 PER SHARE IS MORE THAN FAIR.
YEAH, "PER SHARE" WOULD HAVE BEEN FAIR.
ANYBODY WANT A COPY?

AS NEW OWNER OF THIS COMPANY I HEREBY BAN ALL MEETINGS OVER ONE HOUR. THE DRESS CODE IS CASUAL. STATUS REPORTS ARE OPTIONAL!
NO MORE MISSION STATEMENTS OR "VISIONS." OUR MOTTO IS "HAVE FUN, SATISFY CUSTOMERS, MAKE MONEY."
S. Adams
AND STOCK OPTIONS FOR ALL.
ZZZ
WE CAN FIT FIVE MORE IN THIS CUBICLE IF WE REMOVE THE CHAIR.
3-16 © 1995 United Feature Syndicate, Inc. (NYC)

THE RUMORS ARE DESTROYING OUR PRODUCTIVITY. WE CAN'T WORK WITH ALL THIS UNCERTAINTY.
S. Adams
I PLAN TO BUY PROVEN TECHNOLOGY AND HIRE CONTRACT EMPLOYEES. YOU'LL BE GOPHERS FOR THE CONTRACTORS UNTIL YOU RESIGN IN DISGUST AND HUMILIATION.
IS THERE ANY WAY TO GET BACK TO UNCERTAINTY?
I'LL SEE WHAT I CAN DO.
3-17 © 1995 United Feature Syndicate, Inc. (NYC)

NOW THAT YOU OWN THE COMPANY, WHAT DO YOU PLAN TO DO?
TRIM MIDDLE MANAGEMENT.
S. Adams
I'LL FIRE ANYBODY WHO GIVES ME A DOCUMENT MARKED "FYI." THOSE PEOPLE HAVE TOO MUCH TIME ON THEIR HANDS.
ARE YOU SURE THIS WILL SET ME APART FROM THE OTHER MANAGERS?
YOU'LL BE SURPRISED HOW QUICKLY.
FYI
FYI
FYI
3-18 © 1995 United Feature Syndicate, Inc. (NYC)

SO... OKAY, GREAT...
ALRIGHT THEN...
I'M TRAPPED IN THE MEETING THAT WOULD NOT CONCLUDE!!
S Adams
I'M TOO POLITE TO SAY "WE'RE DONE. PLEASE LEAVE."
LIKE I SAID BEFORE...
OH NO! I MISSED THE WINDOW - HE'S REITERATING!!!
SO... OKAY, GREAT...
ALRIGHT THEN...
3-19
© 1995 United Feature Syndicate, Inc.
MAYBE IF I SHAKE HIS HAND HE'LL LEAVE.
BUT LIKE I SAID BEFORE...
NOOOO OOOO!!
...THEN THERE WAS SORT OF A LONG AWKWARD PAUSE...
SO... OKAY, GREAT...

I HIRED A NEW DIRECTOR OF HUMAN RESOURCES TO HANDLE THE DOWN-SIZING.
S. Adams
I NEEDED SOMEBODY WHO ACTS LIKE A FRIEND BUT SECRETLY DELIGHTS IN THE MISERY OF ALL PEOPLE.
3-20
© 1995 United Feature Syndicate, Inc. (NYC)
WE NEED TO TALK, PAUL. BUT FIRST I'M GOING TO BAT YOUR HEAD AROUND AND SCRATCH YOU.
HEE HEE!! THAT'S SO CUTE!
CATBERT THE HR DIRECTOR
HERE'S THE NEW ORG CHART. MAYBE YOU'RE ON IT AND MAYBE NOT.
S. Adams
OOH! NICE TRY! SO CLOSE. TOO BAD.
3-21
© 1995 United Feature Syndicate, Inc. (NYC)
IT'S FUN TO PLAY WITH THEM BEFORE DOWNSIZING THEM.

COME SEE THE NEW ORG CHART.
S. Adams
OOPS, CHANGED MY MIND!
WHAM!!
3-22
© 1995 United Feature Syndicate, Inc. (NYC)
OUCHIE.
I'M SORE, BUT I'VE NEVER FELT SO FREE.

I'VE DECIDED TO SELL THE COMPANY FOR A HUGE PROFIT. I FOUND SOME VERY DISCRIMINATING BUYERS.
S. Adams
WHEN YOU SAY DISCRIMINATING, YOU MEAN...?
THEY HATE PEOPLE FROM THIS COUNTRY.
3-23 © 1995 United Feature Syndicate, Inc. (NYC)
IT'S OKAY. WE HAVE LAWS TO PROTECT US.
THEY'RE LAZY, BUT AT LEAST THEY'RE FUNNY!
HEE HEE

HOW COULD THE ELBONIANS AFFORD TO BUY THIS COMPANY? THEIR WHOLE COUNTRY IS JUST MUD.
S. Adams
THEY PACKAGED THE MUD AND SOLD IT AS A COSMETIC ON THE "COUCH SHOPPING NETWORK." THEY MADE TRILLIONS.
$119.95
3-24 © 1995 United Feature Syndicate, Inc. (NYC)
AT LEAST THEY KNOW HOW TO MANAGE RESOURCES.
THEY SOLD THEIR ENTIRE COUNTRY IN LITTLE JARS. MOST ELBONIANS PERISHED IN MOLTEN LAVA AT THE EARTH'S CORE.

... BUT BY FAR, THIS COMPUTER IS OUR MOST USER-FRIENDLY.
S. Adams
THE PRE-INSTALLED SOFTWARE HAS ONLY ONE BUTTON. AND WE PRESS IT BEFORE IT LEAVES THE FACTORY.
3-25 © 1995 United Feature Syndicate, Inc. (NYC)
WHAT DOES IT DO?
WHOA! I'M IN OVER MY HEAD. LET ME GIVE YOU THEIR TECH SUPPORT NUMBER.

PLEASE ENTER PHOTOCOPIER ACCESS CODE.
S. Adams
WHAT'S THE CODE FOR THIS MACHINE?
THAT'S PROPRIETARY INFORMATION.
WE WORK FOR THE SAME COMPANY. MY CUBICLE IS DOWN THE HALL.
I HAVE NO WAY OF VERIFYING YOUR CLAIM. ANY-BODY COULD COME IN HERE AND SAY THAT.
ASK ME A QUESTION THAT ONLY AN EMPLOYEE OF THIS COMPANY COULD ANSWER.
OKAY.
© 1995 United Feature Syndicate, Inc.
WHAT IS THE ACCESS CODE FOR THIS COPIER?
3-26
SOB
I JUST HAVE ONE...

IN A WAY, I'M GLAD THE ELBONIANS RUN THIS COMPANY NOW.
S. Adams
AFTER YEARS OF BEING THE ONLY FEMALE ENGINEER I'LL ENJOY WATCHING THE ELBONIANS DISCRIMINATE AGAINST YOU GUYS.
3-27 © 1995 United Feature Syndicate, Inc. (NYC)
CONTINUED...
I DIDN'T REALIZE YOU HAD COFFEE WENCHES IN THIS COUNTRY TOO.
I HOPE YOU DON'T WANT CHILDREN, YORGI.

IN THIS COUNTRY WE HAVE A CUSTOM WHEN MEN ASK WOMEN TO FETCH COFFEE.
S. Adams
STAND UP... THAT'S IT... NOW THIS WILL REALLY SURPRISE YOU.
OH GOD
3-28 © 1995 United Feature Syndicate, Inc. (NYC)
I'VE NEVER SEEN ANYBODY GET KICKED INTO HIS HAT BEFORE.
THAT'S GOTTA HURT.

OUR ELBONIAN OWNERS SOLD THE COMPANY TO OUR BIGGEST COMPETITOR.
S. Adams
OUR MOTTO IS "IF YOU CAN'T BEAT 'EM, JOIN 'EM."
I WONDER WHAT THEIR MOTTO IS.
3-29 © 1995 United Feature Syndicate, Inc. (NYC)
THEIR MOTTO IS "AFTER YOU BEAT 'EM, HUMILIATE 'EM."
IT'S NOT VERY CATCHY.

I BUILT A SPREADSHEET TO COMPARE OUR RELATIVE QUALITIES. I'M AFRAID I'M TWENTY PERCENT TOO GOOD FOR YOU. WE MUST STOP DATING.
S. Adams
NO! LOOK, LIZ, YOU HAVE THE WRONG FORMULA IN THIS COLUMN! THAT MUST MEAN I HAVE HIGHER MATH SKILLS THAN YOU! WE'RE ALMOST EVEN!
3-30 © 1995 United Feature Syndicate, Inc. (NYC)
YOU LEFT THAT ERROR IN THERE INTENTION-ALLY.
MY LAST BATCH OF FLOWERS IS WILTING.

I'D LIKE TO KICK-OFF THE PROJECT WITH THE TRADITIONAL BAD-MOUTHING OF THE GUY WHO WORKED ON THIS BEFORE.
S. Adams
HE'S SO SLIMY THAT SLUGS POUR SALT ON HIM. HIS BRAIN WOULD RATTLE IN A FLEA'S SKULL!
3-31 © 1995 United Feature Syndicate, Inc. (NYC)
OH, AND I'LL NEED YOUR FILES.
FLEAS DON'T HAVE "SKULLS"!!

EACH OF YOU WILL WRITE YOUR OBJECTIVES AND GIVE THEM TO ME.
S. Adams
THEN I WILL SCULPT THESE DISPARATE PIECES OF CLAY INTO AN ELEGANT TAPESTRY WHICH WILL BE OUR BUSINESS PLAN.
4-1 © 1995 United Feature Syndicate, Inc. (NYC)
OUR BUSINESS PLAN WILL BE LIKE A CLAY TAPESTRY?
FEEL FREE TO QUOTE ME.

I'D LIKE YOU GUYS TO CHECK ANNE'S ADVERTISING MATERIALS FOR TECHNICAL ACCURACY.
S. Adams
IS THIS SUPPOSED TO BE FUNNY?
I DON'T GET IT.
I'M ONLY LOOKING FOR TECHNICAL HELP HERE.
HEY! MAYBE YOU COULD SAY SOMETHING ABOUT THOSE WARNING TAGS ON MATTRESSES! NOW THAT WOULD BE FUNNY!
OR HOW ABOUT THE FACT THAT YOU CAN'T LOOK UP SOMETHING IN THE DICTIONARY IF YOU CAN'T SPELL IT? THAT'S FUNNY!
4-2 © 1995 United Feature Syndicate, Inc.
YOU'RE ENGINEERS, NOT COMEDIANS!! I WANT TECHNICAL HELP!!!
THIS GUY HAS AN XP-6. IT SHOULD BE AN XP-7.
THAT'S BETTER.
AND HE SHOULD BE SAYING "I'VE FALLEN AND I CAN'T GET UP."
WHO PICKED THESE COLORS?

MY LAPTOP COMPUTER IS LOCKED UP. CAN YOU HELP?
S. Adams
REMEMBER YOU HAVE TO HOLD IT UPSIDE DOWN AND SHAKE IT TO REBOOT.
OH, THAT'S RIGHT.
4-3 © 1995 United Feature Syndicate, Inc. (NYC)
I WONDER IF HE'LL EVER REALIZE WE GAVE HIM AN "ETCH-A-SKETCH."
DOGBERT THE CONSULTANT
YOUR BEST BET IS TO RELOCATE THE COMPANY TO RUSSIA.
S. Adams
YOU CAN HIRE ENGINEERS FOR TWO CENTS A YEAR!
IS IT DIFFICULT TO WEED OUT THE DUMB ONES?
4-4 © 1995 United Feature Syndicate, Inc. (NYC)
NO. AND THAT LEADS ME INTO THE GOOD NEWS ABOUT THEIR OCCUPATIONAL SAFETY LAWS.
IT'S LIKE HEAVEN!

I WANT TO ASSURE YOU THAT ANY RUMORS YOU'VE HEARD ARE FALSE.
S. Adams
WE ARE NOT PLANNING TO RELOCATE THE COMPANY TO THE SOUTH POLE WHERE EASILY TRAINABLE NATIVE ESKIMOS WILL REPLACE YOU.
© 1995 United Feature Syndicate, Inc. (NYC)
THAT'S GOOD BECAUSE THERE AREN'T ANY ESKIMOS AT THE SOUTH POLE.
EXCUSE ME, I HAVE TO MAKE A PHONE CALL.
4-5

WE'RE OFFERING ATTRACTIVE INCENTIVES TO COMPANIES THAT MOVE TO ELBONIA.
S. Adams
ZERO TAXES, CHEERFUL SLAVE LABOR, AMNESTY FROM ANY INCONVENIENT LAWS, AND ABSOLUTELY NO ENVIRONMENTAL REGULATIONS!
4-6 © 1995 United Feature Syndicate, Inc. (NYC)
IS THAT THE BEST YOU CAN DO?
HERE, USE MY FIRSTBORN SON AS A LAWN ORNAMENT.

TRY THIS LITTLE TRICK TO IMPROVE YOUR CAREER...
S. Adams
ANYTIME YOU WANT SOMETHING YOUR WAY, SIMPLY REFER TO YOUR CEO BY HIS FIRST NAME AND SAY HE GAVE YOU DIRECTIONS DURING YOUR VERY RECENT MEETING.
4-7 © 1995 United Feature Syndicate, Inc. (NYC)
IT'S TOTALLY UNVERIFIABLE. PEOPLE WILL FEAR YOU AND DO AS YOU SAY. YOU'LL RULE WITH AN IRON FIST!
YOU'RE A FUNNY LITTLE DOG.

JUST AS I THOUGHT, MY CUBICLE IS TWO INCHES SMALLER TODAY THAN YESTERDAY!
S. Adams
WE INSTALLED REAL-TIME STATUS ADJUSTERS IN THE CUBICLE WALLS. SENSORS MONITOR YOUR WORK AND ADJUST THE CUBICLE SIZE ACCORDING TO YOUR VALUE.
4-8 © 1995 United Feature Syndicate, Inc. (NYC)
IT'S AMAZING HOW FAST YOU GET USED TO IT.

WE RANKED ALL THE ENGINEERS FROM BEST TO WORST.
WE PLAN TO GET RID OF THE BOTTOM 10%. THAT INCLUDES YOU, WALLY.
S. Adams
YOUR PLAN IS LOGICALLY FLAWED.
IF YOU FIRE THE BOTTOM 10%, YOU'LL STILL HAVE A BOTTOM 10%.
YOU'LL FIRE AND FIRE BUT THERE WILL ALWAYS BE A BOTTOM 10%, UNTIL FINALLY...
© 1995 United Feature Syndicate, Inc.
WHEN LESS THAN TEN PEOPLE ARE LEFT YOU'LL HAVE TO FIRE BODY PARTS INSTEAD OF WHOLE PEOPLE!!!
WE'LL HAVE TORSOS AND GLANDS WANDER-ING AROUND UNABLE TO USE KEYBOARDS... BLOOD AND BILE EVERYWHERE!!!
4-9
HOW'D IT GO?
HE FIRED MY HAIR.

THIS ERGONOMIC KEYBOARD IS OUR FIRST PRODUCT DEVELOPED UNDER THE "BIG Q" PROGRAM.
S. Adams
THE "Q" STANDS FOR QUALITY.
SPEAKING OF Q... IT'S MISSING THE LETTER Q.
4-10 © 1995 United Feature Syndicate, Inc. (NYC)
YOU SOUND JUST LIKE OUR WHINY CUSTOMERS.
I GUESS THE "Q" STANDS FOR "UALITY."

OKAY, SO WE SHIPPED A MILLION KEYBOARDS THAT DON'T HAVE THE LETTER "Q." WHAT DO WE DO?
S. Adams
WE COULD OFFER FREE UPGRADES TO USERS WHO CAN PROVE THEY NEED A "Q."
4-11 © 1995 United Feature Syndicate, Inc. (NYC)
HOW MANY USERS NEED A "Q"?
WELL... THERE'S THE ROYAL FAMILY...

THE PUNDITS IN THE PRESS ARE NAILING US FOR SHIPPING A KEYBOARD WITH NO "Q."
NEWS
S. Adams
IT'S A PUBLIC-RELATIONS FIASCO. OBVIOUSLY, WE NEED AN ENGINEERING SOLUTION.
I'M ON THE CASE.
NEWS
4-12 © 1995 United Feature Syndicate, Inc. (NYC)
USERS COULD USE A GRAPHICS PROGRAM TO DRAW A "Q" IN THE UNLIKELY EVENT THAT THEY NEED ONE.
OR WE COULD REPLACE THE SEMI-COLON; NOBODY USES THEM.

YOU COULD OFFER FREE REPLACEMENTS FOR ALL THE KEYBOARDS YOU SOLD WITH-OUT A "Q," OR YOU COULD BLAME THE MEDIA FOR BLOWING IT OUT OF PROPORTION.
S. Adams
LET'S BLAME THE MEDIA. THEY'LL ADMIT THEY WERE WRONG AND THE WHOLE THING WILL DISAPPEAR.
4-13 © 1995 United Feature Syndicate, Inc. (NYC)
YOU HAVE A BRILLIANT GRASP OF HUMAN NATURE, WALLY.
I KNOW. MY THIRD WIFE ALWAYS SAID THE SAME THING.

DOGBERT THE PR CONSULTANT
YOU SHIPPED KEYBOARDS WITH NO LETTER "Q." THE PUBLIC WANTS SOMEBODY TO TAKE RESPONSI-BILITY.
S. Adams
OOH OOH PICK ME PICK ME!!
4-14 © 1995 United Feature Syndicate, Inc. (NYC)
RESPONSI-BILITY MEANS BLAME.
GREAT... IT'S LIKE THE TIME I GOT BURNED ON THAT "OPPOR-TUNITY" ASSIGNMENT.

STICK TO THE SCRIPT. ACT SINCERE AND BEG YOUR CUSTOMERS TO FORGIVE YOU.
S. Adams
IT WAS WRONG FOR US TO SELL KEYBOARDS WITH NO "Q." WE'RE SORRY. WE'RE MORONS.
4-15 © 1995 United Feature Syndicate, Inc. (NYC)
WE'RE DUMBER THAN SQUIRRELS. WE HEAR VOICES AND DO WHAT THEY COMMAND. I HAVE BROCCOLI IN MY SOCKS.
GOOD WRITING
THANKS

LOOKS LIKE SOMEBODY HAS A JOB INTERVIEW.
SHHH
S. Adams
YOUR RÉSUMÉ IS IMPRESSIVE. I ONLY HAVE ONE QUESTION.
WHAT DO YOU CONSIDER YOUR BIGGEST FAULT?
SOMETIMES I WORK TOO HARD.
GOOD ONE
WHY IS THAT A FAULT?
© 1995 United Feature Syndicate, Inc.
WELL... UH... I WORK SO HARD THAT I FORGET TO EAT AND BATHE FOR DAYS. EVENTUALLY I STARVE TO DEATH AT MY DESK.
4-16
I BECOME A BLOATED, STINKING CORPSE. INSECTS BREED IN MY BODY. I SPREAD DISEASE TO THE ENTIRE COMPANY.
HOW DID IT GO?
THEY WANT SOMEBODY HUNGRIER.

I'M GOING INTO BUSINESS AS A FINANCIAL ADVISOR.
SOUNDS HARD.
S. Adams
IT'S EASY. I'LL TELL ALL MY CLIENTS TO INVEST IN THE "DOGBERT DEFERRED EARNINGS FUND."
4-17 © 1995 United Feature Syndicate, Inc. (NYC)
ISN'T THAT A CONFLICT OF INTEREST?
ONLY IF I SHOW INTEREST IN THE CLIENT.

DOGBERT: FINANCIAL ADVISOR
STOCKS... ANNUITIES... DERIVATIVES... CAPITAL GAINS TAX...
S. Adams
IT'S ALL TOO CONFUSING FOR YOU!! GIVE ME ALL YOUR MONEY NOW OR YOU'LL DIE A PAUPER!! NOW! NOW! BEFORE INTEREST RATES FALL!!
4-18 © 1995 United Feature Syndicate, Inc. (NYC)
WILL THIS REDUCE MY INCOME TAXES?
MORE THAN YOU MIGHT GUESS.

DOGBERT: FINANCIAL ADVISOR
HERE'S A PICTURE OF YOU LIVING IN A DUMPSTER IN TWENTY YEARS.
S. Adams
BUT IF YOU INVEST IN THE "DOGBERT DEFERRED INCOME FUND" TAKE A LOOK AT WHAT YOU COULD OWN SOMEDAY!!
4-19 © 1995 United Feature Syndicate, Inc. (NYC)
I COULD OWN A MANSION?!!
YOU COULD OWN A PHOTOGRAPH.

WE'RE MOVING TO A NEW OFFICE ACROSS TOWN. I VOLUNTEERED TO COORDINATE THE MOVE.
S. Adams
I CONTROL YOUR CUBICLE ASSIGNMENT. NAY, YOUR VERY EXISTENCE. FROM NOW ON YOU WILL REFER TO ME AS "LORD WALLY THE PUPPET MASTER."
4-20 © 1995 United Feature Syndicate, Inc. (NYC)
I DON'T THINK IT'S LEGAL TO ENJOY YOUR WORK THIS MUCH.
I BANISH YOU TO THE CUBICLE CLOSEST TO YOUR BOSS!!
ALLOW ME TO INTRODUCE LOUD HOWARD.
HI!
S. Adams
I WILL MAKE LOUD HOWARD YOUR CUBICLE NEIGHBOR IN THE NEW OFFICE UNLESS YOU GIVE ME YOUR IMMORTAL SOUL!!
NICE DAY!
4-21 © 1995 United Feature Syndicate, Inc. (NYC)
...FORTUNATELY I CONVINCED HIM TO TAKE MY LASER PRINTER INSTEAD...
WHAT DID I SAY THAT SOUNDED LIKE "TELL ME ABOUT YOUR DAY"?

"TO HEAR YOUR URGENT VOICE MAIL MESSAGE PRESS ONE..."
S. Adams
"THIS URGENT MESSAGE IS TO ALL EMPLOYEES. PLEASE DISREGARD THE RUMORS OF A MERGER WITH A HEALTHY COMPANY."
4-22 © 1995 United Feature Syndicate, Inc. (NYC)
NOW SPOOKED, THE HERD STAMPEDES.
RÉSUMÉ!
WHERE'S MY INTERVIEW SUIT??!!

YOU'LL BE PERFORMING A "TURING TEST" ON OUR NEW ARTIFICIAL INTELLIGENCE SOFTWARE.
S. Adams
TRY TO DETERMINE IF THE RESPONSES ON YOUR SCREEN COME FROM OUR COMPUTER OR A HUMAN IN THE NEXT ROOM.
I'LL ASK IT TO WRITE A STRATEGY FOR OUR COMPANY.
"OUR STRATEGY IS TO VISIONIZE QUALITY RESOURCES THAT ENHANCE EARNINGS."
HMM
I'LL ASK IT HOW TO MOTIVATE EMPLOYEES.
4-23 © 1995 United Feature Syndicate, Inc.
"REORGANIZE OFTEN TO IMPROVE FOCUS. REDEFINE WORK AS 'OPPORTUNITY' AND INCREASE IT DAILY. TAKE TIME TO ASK FOR OPINIONS THEN EXPLAIN WHY THEY'RE WRONG."
IT MUST BE A COMPUTER BECAUSE THERE'S NO HUMAN INTELLIGENCE.
UNLESS...
NICE TRY, BOSS.

WE'VE GOT A LOT OF EMPTY CUBICLES BECAUSE OF DOWNSIZING.
S. Adams
I HIRED THE DOGBERT CONSTRUCTION COMPANY TO CONVERT PART OF THE OFFICE INTO PRISON CELLS
WHICH WE'LL LEASE TO THE STATE.
4-24 © 1995 United Feature Syndicate, Inc. (NYC)
SOUNDS LIKE A BIG JOB.
NAH. A LITTLE PAINT, NEW CARPET AND WE'RE THERE.
I DON'T THINK IT'S FAIR TO PUT CONVICTS IN OUR SPARE CUBICLES.
S. Adams
DON'T BE SUCH A BIGOT. THESE PEOPLE HAVE MADE ONE LITTLE MISTAKE. OTHERWISE, THEY'RE JUST LIKE EMPLOYEES.
4-25 © 1995 United Feature Syndicate, Inc. (NYC)
I THINK THERE ARE A FEW DIFFERENCES!
YEAH, THEIR HEALTH PLAN IS BETTER.

HEY, BUDDY, WHAT ARE YOU IN FOR?
S. Adams
UNLIKE YOURSELF, I AM NOT A PRISONER HERE. I CHOOSE TO WORK HERE OF MY OWN FREE WILL!
4-26 © 1995 United Feature Syndicate, Inc. (NYC)
GREAT... I'M IN THE FREAK SECTION.
I LIKE TO WORK.

EFFECTIVE IMMEDIATELY, WE WILL NO LONGER USE OUR SPARE CUBICLES TO HOUSE CONVICTS.
YES!!! OUR OPINIONS MATTERED!
ACTUALLY, IT'S BECAUSE THE PRISONERS COMPLAINED.
I WONDER WHAT HE PLANS TO DO WITH THE SPARE CUBICLES NOW.
S. Adams
4-27 © 1995 United Feature Syndicate, Inc. (NYC)

BAD NEWS IN 1985
WE'RE REPLACING THE COMPANY DOCTOR WITH A REGISTERED NURSE.
BAD NEWS IN 1990
WE FIRED THE NURSE AND PUT THE ASPIRIN AND TOURNIQUETS IN THE VENDING MACHINE.
BAD NEWS IN 1995
WE'VE BEEN ASKED TO INCREASE VENDING MACHINE REVENUE BY FIFTEEN PERCENT.
S. Adams
4-28 © 1995 United Feature Syndicate, Inc. (NYC)

I'M PLANNING TO TURN THE HOUSE INTO A GAMBLING CASINO.
ISN'T THAT ILLEGAL?
NOT IN THE TINY REPUBLIC OF DOGBERTLAND. I SECEDED FROM THE REPRESSIVE HOMELAND THIS MORNING.
I DON'T REMEMBER VOTING ON THAT.
HERE'S YOUR GREEN CARD.
S. Adams
4-29 © 1995 United Feature Syndicate, Inc. (NYC)

LET ME INTRODUCE YOU TO ONE OF OUR ENGINEERS.
S. Adams
KAREN IS OUR NEW VICE PRESIDENT. AND YOU ARE...?
DILBERT: VALUED EMPLOYEE.
I BELIEVE IN OPEN COMMUNICATIONS, DILBERT. FEEL FREE TO TALK ABOUT ANYTHING.
UH-OH
SO, WHAT WERE YOU WORKING ON?
OH-NO
WELL... I WAS JUST SENDING AN E-MAIL TO SOMEBODY WHO SITS BY A WINDOW TO ASK IF IT'S RAINING.
4-30 © 1995 United Feature Syndicate, Inc.
IF IT'S RAINING I'LL FASHION A RAINCOAT FROM A LARGE TRASH BAG.
WATCH.
THREE HOLES AND YOU'RE READY TO GO!
ARE YOU PLANNING TO GO OUT AT LUNCH?
ONLY IF IT RAINS.

I THINK THE BEST WAY TO PURSUE MY GOAL OF WORLD DOMINATION IS TO BECOME A TALK RADIO HOST.
I'LL PROMOTE MY UNIQUE CONSERVATIVE VIEW-POINT THAT PEOPLE ARE IDIOTS WHO DESERVE TO BE MOCKED.
WON'T PEOPLE SHOW YOUR VIEWPOINT TO BE FLAWED BY VIRTUE OF THEIR INTELLIGENT QUESTIONS?
LIKE THAT ONE?
S. Adams
5-1 © 1995 United Feature Syndicate, Inc. (NYC)

DOGBERT'S TALK RADIO
I'M THE SMARTEST CREATURE IN THE UNIVERSE AND YOU ARE ALL DOLTS.
TODAY I'M TAKING CALLS FROM PEOPLE WHO THINK THEY UNDERSTAND COMPLEX ISSUES BECAUSE THEY WATCH "CROSSFIRE" ON CNN.
"... SO WHY NOT PUT ALL POOR PEOPLE IN ORPHANAGES?"
PUT YOUR HEAD UP TO THE SPEAKER, BOB.
S. Adams
5-2 © 1995 United Feature Syndicate, Inc. (NYC)

TODAY WE'RE TALKING ABOUT SEX AFTER MARRIAGE. MANY LIBERALS SUPPORT THIS DEPRAVED PRACTICE BUT I DO NOT.
IT CAN LEAD TO HEAD-ACHES, FATIGUE AND UNWANTED FAMILY MEMBERS WHO BECOME CONSULTANTS.
"WOULDN'T YOUR PHILOSOPHY LEAD TO THE EXTINCTION OF MANKIND?"
CRY ME A RIVER, LIBERAL.
S. Adams
5-3 © 1995 United Feature Syndicate, Inc. (NYC)

WELCOME TO THE DOGBERT SHOW. TODAY I TALK ABOUT GETTING GOVERNMENT OFF OUR BACKS.
I DREAM OF A WORLD WHERE SOMEDAY YOU CAN BUY LIQUOR, CIGARETTES AND FIREARMS AT A DRIVE-THRU WINDOW AND USE THEM ALL BEFORE YOU GET HOME.
BASICALLY, ANYTHING THAT GETS RID OF PEOPLE IS OKAY WITH ME. BUT BEFORE YOU GO, BUY MY NEW BOOK...
S. Adams
5-4 © 1995 United Feature Syndicate, Inc. (NYC)

MY HOBBY IS GEOGRAPHY. WOULD YOU SIGN MY BOOK TO EACH OF THE CONTINENTS BY NAME?
ARE YOU AWARE THAT MY BOOK RECOMMENDS A TWIRLING WEDGIE FOR PEOPLE WHO ASK FOR TOO MUCH?
WE FIND THE LINE MOVES FASTER IF I DO THIS TO THE FIRST CUSTOMER.
S. Adams
5-5 © 1995 United Feature Syndicate, Inc. (NYC)

I'M RETIRING FROM MY MEDIA EMPIRE AND PUTTING MY VAST WEALTH INTO REAL ESTATE.
MY PLAN IS TO BUY ALL THE PROPERTY ON EARTH AND EVICT EVERYBODY WHO DOESN'T AGREE TO BE MY PUPPET.
CAN I BE KERMIT?
THAT'S A "MUPPET." IT'S ALL SPELLED OUT IN YOUR LEASE.
S. Adams
5-6 © 1995 United Feature Syndicate, Inc. (NYC)

THE 7 HABITS OF
HIGHLY DEFECTIVE PEOPLE
OW!
S. ADAMS
1. IGNORE ANY SIGNS OF DISCOMFORT IN OTHERS.
BUT HEY, I'VE BEEN DOING ALL OF THE TALKING.
2. USE HUMOR TO BELITTLE PEOPLE IN PUBLIC.
OUR NEWEST TEAM MEMBER HAS MOVIE STAR LOOKS. SPECIFICALLY, LASSIE.
3. TREAT ALL COMPLAINTS AS THE COMPLAINER'S FAULT.
YOU DON'T MOTIVATE ME.
MAYBE YOU SHOULD SEE A THERAPIST.
4. SHOW UP LATE AND RAISE CONTROVERSIAL ISSUES.
I THINK WE SHOULD LICENSE "BARNEY" AS OUR MASCOT.
© 1995 United Feature Syndicate, Inc.
5-7
5. GIVE ADVICE ON THINGS YOU DON'T UNDERSTAND.
TRY WRITING SOME ASSEMBLY LINE CODE HERE.
6. USE COMPLIMENTS TO SHOW YOUR PREJUDICES.
OOH, NICE CRISP PHOTO-COPY, ALICE. I DON'T THINK A MAN COULD HAVE DONE IT BETTER!
7. THINK THE COMICS ARE NOT ABOUT YOU
HEE HEE! LOOK AT THE HAIR ON THAT GUY!

WHY IS EVERYBODY PUTTING SIGNS ON THEIR CUBICLES?
WE THOUGHT IT WOULD BE CLASSY TO NAME OUR CUBICLES THE SAME WAY WE NAME CONFERENCE ROOMS.
I KNOW THERE'S A CATCH... BUT WHAT?
MENENDEZ ROOMS
O.J. ROOM
S. Adams
5/8 © 1995 United Feature Syndicate, Inc. (NYC)

I'M SO LUCKY TO BE DATING YOU, LIZ. YOU'RE AT LEAST AN EIGHT.
YOU'RE A TEN.
ARE WE USING THE SAME SCALE?
TEN IS THE NUMBER OF SECONDS IT WOULD TAKE TO REPLACE YOU.
S. Adams
5/9 © 1995 United Feature Syndicate, Inc. (NYC)

TO: ALL USERS
FROM: NETWORK ADMIN
PLEASE REFRAIN FROM FRIVOLOUS E-MAIL. IT BOGS DOWN THE NET-WORK.
TO: NETWORK ADMIN
FROM: DILBERT
CC: ALL USERS
I AGREE!
HAVE YOU NOTICED THERE'S TOO MUCH COMMUNICATION IN THE WORLD, DOGBERT?
YEAH, EVERY DAY AT ABOUT THIS TIME.
S. Adams
5/10 © 1995 United Feature Syndicate, Inc. (NYC)

WE COULD SIMPLY DIVIDE THE CHECK BY THREE...
UH-OH. ENGINEERS.
S. Adams
BUT THAT WOULD RESULT IN AN UNPOPULAR SUBSIDY OF WALLY'S SALMON. DOES ANYBODY HAVE A CALCULATOR-WATCH?
5/11 © 1995 United Feature Syndicate, Inc. (NYC)
HOURS LATER
THIS IS THE TIE-BREAKER ROUND OF WATER TO DECIDE IF YOU GET 13% OR 13.5%.
RRRR
TODAY WE HAVE A MOTIVATIONAL SPEAKER FROM THE "DISCOUNT SPEAKERS BUREAU."
S. Adams
YOU SHOULD, LIKE, WORK HARDER... OTHERWISE YOU MIGHT GET FIRED. ANY QUESTIONS?
5/12 © 1995 United Feature Syndicate, Inc. (NYC)
WOULD WE GET BONUSES FOR WORKING HARDER?
THIS MUST BE THE SLOW CLASS.

I'M GOING TO INTERVIEW SUCCESSFUL PEOPLE AND WRITE A BOOK OF THEIR TIPS. I'LL START WITH YOU, DOGBERT.
S. Adams
SET YOUR ALARM CLOCK TO GO OFF EVERY HOUR. KEEP A BIG VAT OF "JELL-O" BY THE BED. WHEN THE ALARM GOES OFF, STICK YOUR HEAD IN THE "JELL-O" AND YELL "BOY, I'M TIRED!"
5/13 © 1995 United Feature Syndicate, Inc. (NYC)
THANKS!
BEWARE THE ADVICE OF SUCCESSFUL PEOPLE; THEY DO NOT SEEK COMPANY.

WRITE UP YOUR ACCOMPLISHMENTS SO I CAN DECIDE WHO GETS RAISES THIS YEAR.
ARE YOU SAYING OUR RAISES WILL DEPEND ON OUR ABILITY TO LIE ABOUT OUR ACHIEVEMENTS?
NO, THERE'S ALSO FAVORITISM.
AND DON'T FORGET THE IMPORTANCE OF MINIMIZING THE ACCOMPLISHMENTS OF OTHERS.
"THIS YEAR I SAVED A BILLION DOLLARS IN WAYS WHICH ARE IMPOSSIBLE TO VERIFY."
"WHILE THE OTHERS PLOTTED AGAINST YOU, I WAS APPLYING AN INVISIBLE RUST INHIBITOR TO YOUR CAR."
I CAN DROP THOSE OFF FOR YOU.
THANKS.
HAVE YOU NOTICED SHE'S THE ONLY ONE WHO EVER GETS A RAISE?
IT'S AS IF SHE HAS THE ACCOMPLISHMENTS OF THREE PEOPLE.
S.Adams
© 1995 United Feature Syndicate, Inc.
5-14

WHO NEEDS TO SIGN MY BUSINESS CASE TO BUY A WEB SERVER?
HMM... THIS CROSSES ALL DEPARTMENTS. I FEAR IT. GET THE APPROVAL OF EVERY DIRECTOR, EVERY VP, EVERY EVP, PLUS GRIFFIN.
S. Adams
5/15 © 1995 United Feature Syndicate, Inc. (NYC)
DO YOU MEAN TED GRIFFIN IN FINANCE OR THE MYTHICAL GRIFFIN BEAST THAT'S HALF EAGLE, HALF LION?
WHICHEVER IS HARDER.
I COULD GIVE YOU MARKETING'S APPROVAL RIGHT NOW...
S. Adams
OR I COULD FLEX MY VICE PRESIDENTIAL POWER AND SEND YOU TO GATHER MORE USELESS DATA... MY EGO WOULD EXPAND AND I'D BE A MAJOR STALLION WITH MY WIFE TONIGHT.
5/16 © 1995 United Feature Syndicate, Inc. (NYC)
DO YOU THINK YOU CAN TOP THAT?
I'LL TRY, SIR. WHAT'S YOUR WIFE'S ADDRESS?
I NEED YOUR APPROVAL ON MY BUSINESS CASE, TOM.
S. Adams
I'LL WEDGE IT IN HERE SO YOU CAN CLAIM YOU NEVER SAW IT WHEN I ASK ABOUT IT NEXT WEEK.
THANKS
5/17 © 1995 United Feature Syndicate, Inc. (NYC)
THE WEIRD PART IS THAT I CAN FEEL PRODUCTIVE EVEN WHEN I'M DOOMED.

TODAY I DISTRIBUTED 36 COPIES OF MY BUSINESS CASE TO VARIOUS MANAGERS FOR APPROVAL.
BY MY COUNT, 20 ARE BEING MISPLACED, 6 MANAGERS WILL TRY TO KILL IT FOR PERSONAL GAIN AND 10 WILL COME BACK WITH IRRELEVANT QUESTIONS.
WHEN I DIE I WANT TO BE BURIED, NOT CREMATED, SO I CAN AT LEAST MAKE ONE LASTING IMPRESSION ON THE EARTH.
I WAS PLANNING TO MAIL YOUR CORPSE TO SOMEBODY I DON'T LIKE.
S. Adams
5/18 © 1995 United Feature Syndicate, Inc. (NYC)
WE NEED TO BOOST OUR RETURN-ON-ASSETS RATIO.
LET'S ELIMINATE THE SECURITY DEPARTMENT. THAT WOULD CUT EXPENSES WHILE ALLOWING FOR A BRISK REDUCTION IN ASSETS.
WHEN ARE YOU PLANNING TO TELL HIM YOU WERE JOKING?
AFTER I FURNISH MY DEN.
S. Adams
5/19 © 1995 United Feature Syndicate, Inc. (NYC)

YOU NEVER ANSWERED MY E-MAIL.
MY SECRETARY IS OUT, SO THERE'S NOBODY TO PRINT MY E-MAIL FOR ME. BRING ME YOUR MESSAGE ON HARDCOPY.
I WAS OUT OF PAPYRUS SO I CHISELED MY MESSAGE ON A LITTLE PYRAMID.
DID HE WORK ALONE OR WERE UFOs INVOLVED?
S. Adams
5/20 © 1995 United Feature Syndicate, Inc. (NYC)

HERE'S THE COMPANY VISION AND BUSINESS PLAN.
S. Adams
"VISION: EMPOWERED EMPLOYEES WORKING TOWARD A COMMON PLAN."
SOUNDS GOOD.
BUT THE BUSINESS PLAN IS BLANK.
IT'S CONFIDENTIAL.
HOW AM I SUPPOSED TO KNOW WHAT TO DO?
I'LL YELL AT YOU IF YOU DO THE WRONG THING.
I THOUGHT I WAS EMPOWERED.
DON'T BE SO LITERAL.
© 1995 United Feature Syndicate, Inc.
5-21
I'LL JUST KEEP DOING WHAT I WAS DOING.
NO!!! YOU FOOL!!!
WE'RE DOOMED, AREN'T WE?
I DON'T KNOW. I HAVEN'T SEEN THE PLAN.

OUR POLICY IS TO EMPLOY ONLY THE BEST TECHNICAL PROFESSIONALS.
QUESTION.
S. Adams
ISN'T IT ALSO OUR POLICY TO BASE SALARIES ON THE INDUSTRY AVERAGE?
5/22 © 1995 United Feature Syndicate, Inc. (NYC)
RIGHT. WE LIKE THEM BRIGHT BUT CLUELESS.
I FEEL SORRY FOR PEOPLE LIKE THAT.

MY SALARY DEPENDS ON YOUR OPINION OF MY WORK. BUT YOU HAVE NO INTEREST IN UNDERSTANDING WHAT I DO, SO...
S. Adams
I HIRED THE DOGBERT PUBLIC RELATIONS FIRM TO HYPE MY PERFORMANCE AND GET ME A BIG RAISE.
5/23 © 1995 United Feature Syndicate, Inc. (NYC)
PRESS RELEASE: ENGINEER CURES CANCER WHILE SAVING BABY FROM BURNING BUILDING
THAT'S NOT IN HIS OBJECTIVES.

YOU CAN CREATE THE ILLUSION THAT YOU WORK LONG HOURS BY LEAVING VOICE MAILS FOR YOUR BOSS AT 4 A.M.
S. Adams
HI, THIS IS DILBERT. IT'S 4 A.M. AND I'M IN MY UNDERWEAR AND I THOUGHT OF YOU... OOPS... ERASE... OOPS...
BEEP BEEP
5/24 © 1995 United Feature Syndicate, Inc. (NYC)
DID YOU JUST SEND AN OBSCENE MESSAGE TO YOUR BOSS?
NO... I THINK I HIT THE GROUP CODE.

TELL ME YOUR GREATEST ACCOMPLISHMENTS AT WORK. I'LL USE THAT TO HYPE YOU UP WITH YOUR BOSS SO YOU GET A BIG RAISE.
S. Adams
I WROTE A DRAFT OF A WHITE PAPER ON A STRAWMAN PROCESS TO REENGINEER OUR PRODUCT PROCESS.
5/25 © 1995 United Feature Syndicate, Inc. (NYC)
AND WHAT WAS THE IMPACT OF THAT WORK?
I THINK SOME OWLS LOST THEIR WOODLAND HABITATS.
YOU MUST LEARN TO USE YOUR BOSS'S IGNORANCE TO YOUR ADVANTAGE.
S. Adams
FIND OUT WHAT IMPRESSES HIM AND LIST IT ON YOUR ACCOMPLISHMENTS.
5/26 © 1995 United Feature Syndicate, Inc. (NYC)
YOU'RE THE ACTOR IN THE "BARNEY" SUIT?!! I LOVE THAT GUY!
DON'T TELL ANYBODY MY SECRET IDENTITY.

IN MY DREAM I FLOAT OVER FIELDS OF HEATHER.
Hi! I'M Heather
S. Adams
THE FLYING DREAM ALWAYS PREDICTS AN IMPORTANT CHANGE. I FEEL THAT MY FREE-DOM WILL SOON INCREASE.
5/27 © 1995 United Feature Syndicate, Inc. (NYC)
DOES SOMEBODY ELSE HAVE A QUESTION FOR OUR NEW CEO?
MY FINGER IS STUCK.

I'M PUTTING YOU IN CHARGE OF PROJECT "BIFF."
DILBERT
"BIFF" STANDS FOR "BIG IMPROVEMENTS FOR FREE."
YOUR JOB IS TO RECOMMEND WAYS TO INCREASE PROFITS WITHOUT SPENDING MONEY OR CHANGING ANYTHING.
YOU HAVE TO SPEND MONEY TO MAKE MONEY.
IF WE HAD MONEY TO SPEND WE WOULDN'T NEED TO MAKE MONEY.
DUH
S. Adams
THE POINT IS THAT YOU CAN MAKE MORE MONEY THAN YOU SPEND.
5-28 © 1995 United Feature Syndicate, Inc.
I'M NOT FOLLOWING YOUR SO-CALLED "POINT."
LOGICALLY, ANYTHING I DON'T UNDERSTAND IS UNIMPORTANT.
HAVE YOUR REPORT TOMORROW.
SO, YOU RECOMMEND... REPLACING ALL MANAGERS WITH LAVA LAMPS.
HERE'S A FEW BUCKS FOR THE LAVA LAMPS.

I'VE DECIDED TO BE MORE OF A HANDS-ON MANAGER.
MOVE THE MOUSE... UP... UP... OVER... MORE... NOW CLICK IT!! CLICK IT!!
S. Adams
NO!!! YOU FOOL!!!
THIS HAS "LONG DAY" WRITTEN ALL OVER IT.
5/29 © 1995 United Feature Syndicate, Inc. (NYC)
HAVE YOU TAKEN THE MANDATORY TRAINING FOR BUSINESS ETHICS?
NO. BUT IF YOU SAY I DID THEN YOU'LL SAVE SOME MONEY ON TRAINING WHICH YOU CAN SPEND TO DECORATE YOUR OFFICE.
S. Adams
LUCKILY, I HAVEN'T TAKEN THE TRAINING MYSELF.
I HEAR IT'S MOSTLY COMMON SENSE ANY-WAY.
5/30 © 1995 United Feature Syndicate, Inc. (NYC)

HEY! THAT LITTLE STUFFED DOLL LOOKS JUST LIKE ME!
IT GIVES ME AN EMOTIONAL LIFT TO HAVE YOUR LIKENESS NEARBY.
S. Adams
I NEVER REALIZED WHAT HE THOUGHT OF ME.
STOP DROPPING IN LIKE THAT!!
WHACK!
5/31 © 1995 United Feature Syndicate, Inc. (NYC)

MY CELLULAR PHONE AND LAPTOP COMPUTER ALLOW ME TO WORK ANY TIME AND ANYPLACE...
S. Adams
WHILE DRIVING?
TOO DANGEROUS
IN RESTAURANTS?
TOO RUDE
OUTDOORS?
NOPE.
6/1 © 1995 United Feature Syndicate, Inc. (NYC)
BASICALLY, YOU LUG THEM AROUND AND WORRY THAT THEY'LL GET STOLEN OR BROKEN.
STOP IT. YOU'RE SCARING THEM.

WHAT'S THE HAT FOR, WALLY?
IT'S A NEW SAFETY RULE. I THINK IT'S STUPID.
S. Adams
THE E-MAIL FROM HUMAN RESOURCES SAID ALL SHORT EMPLOYEES MUST WEAR THESE TO IMPROVE VISIBILITY WHILE IN THE CUBICLE AISLES.
6/2 © 1995 United Feature Syndicate, Inc. (NYC)
HR SHOULD CHANGE THEIR PASSWORD ONCE IN A WHILE.
I'LL BET WE CAN MAKE HIM WEAR ALUMINUM FOIL PANTS.

HERE'S YOUR LATEST BUDGET CUTS. BUT PLEASE DON'T KILL THE MESSENGER FROM FINANCE, HA HA!!
S. Adams
I RECOMMENDED A 20% CUT. A QUICK GLANCE AROUND THE ROOM TELLS ME YOU'RE NOT ON THE SUCCESS VECTOR ANYHOO, SO NOTHING LOST.
6/3 © 1995 United Feature Syndicate, Inc. (NYC)
TOUGH ROOM.

YOUR COMPANY MAKES AN ATTRACTIVE LITTLE PRODUCT, JIM.
BUT WE'VE DECIDED TO GO WITH A VENDOR WHOSE PRODUCT ACTUALLY WORKS.
S.Adams
FOOLS!!! I'LL CRUSH YOU!!!
I'LL TELL YOUR BOSS YOU MADE A STUPID DECISION!! YOUR CAREERS WILL BE RUINED AND I'LL GET THE CONTRACT ANYWAY!!
YOU CAN'T SCARE US! DO YOU THINK OUR BOSS WILL BELIEVE A VENDOR OVER HIS OWN LOYAL EMPLOYEES?
© 1995 United Feature Syndicate, Inc.
MUST... KEEP... A... STRAIGHT... FACE...
6-4
HA HA HA HA HA HA HA HA
WE'LL TAKE A MILLION UNITS.
TAKE TWO MILLION AND I'LL SEE THAT YOU GET NICE RAISES.

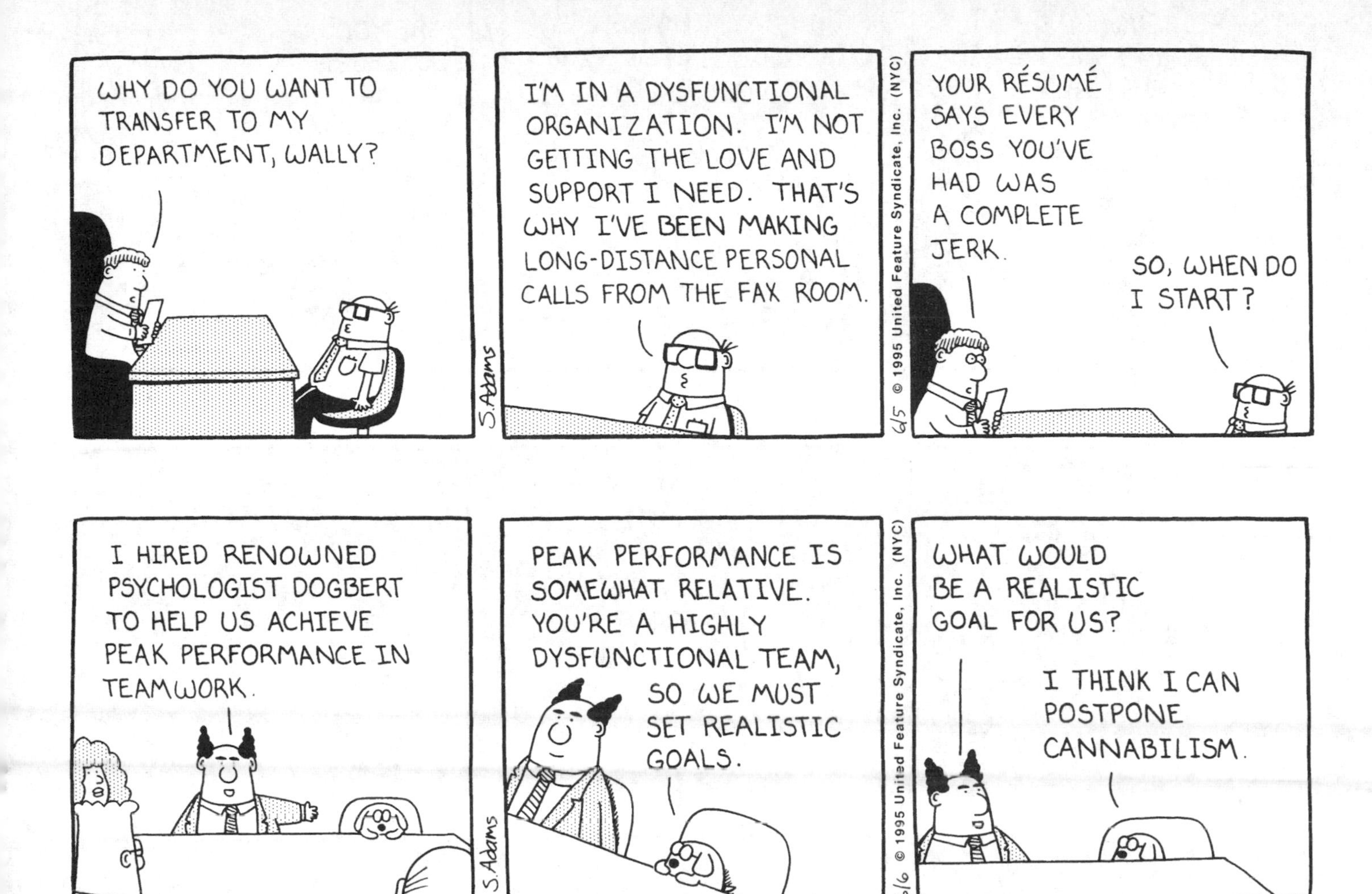
WHY DO YOU WANT TO TRANSFER TO MY DEPARTMENT, WALLY?
I'M IN A DYSFUNCTIONAL ORGANIZATION. I'M NOT GETTING THE LOVE AND SUPPORT I NEED. THAT'S WHY I'VE BEEN MAKING LONG-DISTANCE PERSONAL CALLS FROM THE FAX ROOM.
YOUR RÉSUMÉ SAYS EVERY BOSS YOU'VE HAD WAS A COMPLETE JERK.
SO, WHEN DO I START?
S. Adams
6/5 © 1995 United Feature Syndicate, Inc. (NYC)
I HIRED RENOWNED PSYCHOLOGIST DOGBERT TO HELP US ACHIEVE PEAK PERFORMANCE IN TEAMWORK.
PEAK PERFORMANCE IS SOMEWHAT RELATIVE. YOU'RE A HIGHLY DYSFUNCTIONAL TEAM,
SO WE MUST SET REALISTIC GOALS.
WHAT WOULD BE A REALISTIC GOAL FOR US?
I THINK I CAN POSTPONE CANNABILISM.
S. Adams
6/6 © 1995 United Feature Syndicate, Inc. (NYC)

DYSFUNCTIONAL TEAM...
I'D LIKE EVERYBODY TO TURN TO THE RIGHT AND SAY WHAT YOU ADMIRE ABOUT THAT PERSON.
I ADMIRE YOUR LEATHERY SKIN, ALICE.
I ADMIRE YOUR ABILITY TO FIGURE OUT WHICH SIDE IS YOUR RIGHT IN ONLY TWO TRIES.
I ADMIRE YOUR ABILITY TO GET PAID FOR THIS.
DESPITE THE FACT YOUR FACE SCARES CHILDREN, I ADMIRE YOUR CO-WORKERS.
S. Adams
6/7 © 1995 United Feature Syndicate, Inc. (NYC)

IN THIS TEAM-BUILDING EXERCISE YOU WILL MAKE PAPER DOLLS WHILE BLINDFOLDED.
S. Adams
THIS MAY SEEM ABSURD. BUT SOON, COGNITIVE DISSONANCE WILL SET IN AND YOU'LL CRY AND HUG AND THINK YOU LEARNED SOMETHING.
6/8 © 1995 United Feature Syndicate, Inc. (NYC)
ARE YOU SURE WE'LL CRY AND HUG?
ACTUALLY, HUGGING IS IFFY.
DYSFUNCTIONAL TEAM...
I'D LIKE EACH OF YOU TO TELL THE TEAM WHAT YOU LEARNED IN MY WORKSHOP.
S. Adams
I LEARNED TO LISTEN WITH MY HEART. I GAINED RESPECT FOR OTHERS. I UNDERSTAND SANSKRIT. I GOT MY HAM RADIO LICENSE. I CAN DIVIDE BY ZERO...
6/9 © 1995 United Feature Syndicate, Inc. (NYC)
I LOVE GOING FIRST.
YOU'VE GOT TO INCREASE THE BUDGET FOR TRAINING!
S. Adams
IF I TRAIN YOU, THEN WOULDN'T YOU JUST LEAVE THE COMPANY TO MAKE MORE MONEY WORKING FOR OUR COMPETITOR?
6/10 © 1995 United Feature Syndicate, Inc. (NYC)
I GUESS THERE IS A DOWN-SIDE.
AND THE DOWNSIDE WOULD BE...?

LET'S GO AROUND THE CIRCLE AND SHARE WHAT WE LEARNED IN THE THREE-DAY WORKSHOP.
TEAM
S. Adams
AT FIRST I THOUGHT IT WAS A WASTE OF OUR TRAINING BUDGET...
THEN YOU ASKED US TO FORM TEAMS AND MAKE PAPER AIRPLANES WHILE BLINDFOLDED...
I DON'T KNOW IF IT WAS BECAUSE OF THE DARKNESS OR THE WAY WE SHARED OUR THOUGHTS ABOUT FLIGHT...
BUT SUDDENLY I FOUND UNCONDITIONAL LOVE FOR MY CO-WORKERS.
BE THEY ACCOUNTANTS, BE THEY MARKETEERS OR BE THEY SECRETARIES.
© 1995 United Feature Syndicate, Inc.
6-11
AS A RESULT, I'VE BECOME A COMPETITIVE LION, EAGER TO POUNCE ON MY WORKLOAD AND INCREASE STOCK-HOLDER VALUES!!
THANK YOU, WALLY.
DILBERT, WHAT DID YOU LEARN?
I LEARNED THAT YOU SHOULDN'T PUT A LITTLE ERASER-PILOT IN YOUR PAPER AIRPLANE.
SOMEBODY NEEDS A GROUP HUG!

HAVE FUN WORKING. I'M OFF TO THE TWO-WEEK MANAGEMENT RETREAT IN THE MOUNTAINS.
S. Adams
IT'S SO SAD YOU CAN'T COME. I GUESS THERE ISN'T ROOM AT THE FOUR-STAR HOTEL.
6/12 © 1995 United Feature Syndicate, Inc. (NYC)
NOW I KNOW WHY IT'S CALLED A RETREAT.

HELLO, IS THIS THE MOUNTAIN RESORT WHERE ALL OUR EXECUTIVES ARE HAVING A RETREAT?
S. Adams
IS IT TRUE THAT LOUD NOISES CAN CAUSE AVALANCHES?
IF YOU SEE MY BOSS, TELL HIM I SAID...
6/13 © 1995 United Feature Syndicate, Inc. (NYC)
HI!!

GREAT NEWS! I'VE REENGINEERED YOUR JOB TO MAKE YOU MORE FULFILLED!
S. Adams
YOU'LL NO LONGER BE LIMITED TO ONE LITTLE PART OF THE VALUE CHAIN. YOU'LL BE INVOLVED IN ALL STAGES OF PRODUCTION!
6/14 © 1995 United Feature Syndicate, Inc. (NYC)
OH LORD, YOU FIRED ALL THE SECRETARIES!!
DUST MY CREDENZA.

LACKING CLERICAL SUPPORT, THE HIGHLY TRAINED, HIGHLY PAID PROFESSIONALS LINE UP AT THE COPIER.
THEIR AMAZING ANALYTICAL SKILLS ARE SQUANDERED IN THIS MINDLESS TASK.
NO... IT LOOKS LIKE THE "TONER" LIGHT DOESN'T TURN OFF IF YOU WAIT.
LET'S GIVE IT ANOTHER FIVE MINUTES.
S. Adams
6/15 © 1995 United Feature Syndicate, Inc. (NYC)

MY NEW GOAL, BOB, IS TO BE THE NEXT HEAVY-WEIGHT BOXING CHAMPION OF THE WORLD!!
DON'T LET ANYBODY EVER TELL YOU THAT YOU'RE TOO SMALL OR TOO SLOW OR TOO UNCOORDINATED.
OR TOO CLUELESS.
EXACTLY! NOW YOU'RE CATCHING ON.
S. Adams
6/16 © 1995 United Feature Syndicate, Inc. (NYC)

I SEE SIGNS OF PRODUCTIVITY HERE. I'M MOVING YOU TO ANOTHER CUBICLE.
DILBERT
YOUR PHONE AND COMPUTER WILL BE DISCONNECTED FOR WEEKS. YOUR FILES WILL BE BOXED AND LOST.
GOOD LORD, YOU'VE ABANDONED ALL PRETENSE OF BEING ON OUR SIDE!!
LOSER
S. Adams
6/17 © 1995 United Feature Syndicate, Inc. (NYC)

IVE BEEN INVITED TO BE A GUEST ON "CROSSFIRE" ON CNN.
S. Adams
I'M THE ONLY CREATURE ON EARTH WHO HASN'T ALREADY BEEN ON TELEVISION.
CAN YOU TEACH ME HOW TO DEBATE ON TELEVISION, DOGBERT?
OKAY
FIRST, RATBERT, ASSUME EVERYBODY HAS THE SAME DESIRES AND EXPERIENCES AS YOU.
ABSORB ABSORB
THEREFORE, IF THEY DISAGREE WITH YOU THEY MUST BE STUPID.
© 1995 United Feature Syndicate, Inc.
6-18
I THINK YOU'RE OVER-SIMPLIFYING, DOGBERT.
WHAT WAS THAT OPINION, RATBERT?
STUPID!
YOU'RE READY FOR "CROSSFIRE," RATBERT.
I USUALLY LIKE THE SAME MOVIES AS THE FAT ONE.

I'VE BEEN HIRED BY THE FINANCE DEPARTMENT TO HELP CUT SPENDING.
S. Adams
I'LL BE STUDYING YOUR EVERY MOVE AND LOOKING FOR WASTE AND INEFFICIENCY.
6/19 © 1995 United Feature Syndicate, Inc. (NYC)
THOSE WORDS IN BOLDFACE LOOK LIKE THEY'RE SUCKING UP THE OL' ELECTRICITY.

I'M FROM THE FINANCE DEPARTMENT. I'M HERE TO REDUCE COSTS.
S. Adams
IT MIGHT SEEM LIKE ALL I DO IS COME UP WITH SHORT-SIGHTED WAYS TO SAVE MONEY WHILE MAKING YOUR JOB HARDER. BUT THERE'S ANOTHER SIDE TO THIS STORY.
6/20 © 1995 United Feature Syndicate, Inc. (NYC)
AND THAT WOULD BE...?
I FORGET.

THE FINANCE DEPARTMENT HAS ANALYZED YOUR COMPUTING NEEDS AND DECIDED TO GIVE YOU A 286 PC.
S. Adams
THAT SHOULD BE SUFFICIENT FOR THE 3D-RENDERING YOU NEED TO DO.
6/21 © 1995 United Feature Syndicate, Inc. (NYC)
BESIDES, HOW MANY TIMES ARE YOU GOING TO DO 3D-RENDERING IN YOUR CAREER?
ONCE, IF I HURRY.

I RECOMMEND STANDARDIZING ON ONE TYPE OF COMPUTER FOR THE OFFICE.
S. Adams
WE MUST IDENTIFY AND ELIMINATE THE DEVIANT USERS OF MACINTOSH, UNIX AND ... GOD HELP US... OS/2 WARP.
6/22 © 1995 United Feature Syndicate, Inc. (NYC)
THE HOLY WARS BEGIN
DON'T LIE TO ME, GUSTAV! YOU'RE A STINKIN' MAC USER!!

MISTER CATBERT, THE COMPANY IS TRYING TO FORCE ME TO USE A DIFFERENT KIND OF COMPUTER.
S. Adams
YOU'RE THE HUMAN RESOURCES DIRECTOR. WHAT ARE YOU DOING TO STOP THIS RELIGIOUS PERSECUTION ??! WHAT EVER HAPPENED TO "DIVERSITY"??
6/23 © 1995 United Feature Syndicate, Inc. (NYC)
THE LONGER YOU VERK HERE, DIVERSE IT GETS.
NEXT.

COMPUTER HOLY WARS
HOLD IT RIGHT THERE, BUDDY.
S. Adams
THAT SCRUFFY BEARD ... THOSE SUSPENDERS ... THAT SMUG EXPRESSION ...
6/24 © 1995 United Feature Syndicate, Inc. (NYC)
YOU'RE ONE OF THOSE CONDESCENDING UNIX COMPUTER USERS!
HERE'S A NICKEL, KID. GET YOURSELF A BETTER COMPUTER.

TAKE CARE OF THIS, ALICE.
"TAKE CARE OF THIS"? THIS WOULD DOUBLE MY WORKLOAD.
S. Adams
I'VE ALREADY GOT SO MANY PROJECTS THAT I CAN'T DO ANYTHING USEFUL WITH ANY OF THEM.
BUT IF SUCCESS IS IMPOSSIBLE THEN...
I'M...FREE.
FREE! FREE! HA HA HA HA HA
© 1995 United Feature Syndicate, Inc.
6-25
THE RESULT WILL BE THE SAME NO MATTER WHAT I DO! YES YES YES
HONK HONK!
MOVING ALONG...WE NEED TO INVENTORY OUR OFFICE EQUIP-MENT.
SOUNDS LIKE A JOB FOR ALICE.

I ASKED SAINT DOGBERT TO MEDIATE OUR DISPUTE OVER WHAT KIND OF COMPUTERS ARE ALLOWED HERE.
S. Adams
I SHALL GO TO THE DESERT AND SEEK ENLIGHTENMENT. WHEN I RETURN I WILL REVEAL THE TRUE PATH OF COMPUTING.
6/26 © 1995 United Feature Syndicate, Inc. (NYC)
PALM SPRINGS
YOU CALL THIS AN ENDORSEMENT CONTRACT?! GO TO THE END OF THE LINE!

ALICE, I WANT YOU TO BENCHMARK THESE WORLD-CLASS COMPANIES. FIND OUT HOW WE COMPARE.
S. Adams
I'M BETTING THEY DON'T MAKE VERBS OUT OF NOUNS. AND I'LL BET THEY DON'T ASSIGN ENGINEERS TO DO FIELD RESEARCH.
6/27 © 1995 United Feature Syndicate, Inc. (NYC)
DO YOU GUYS HAVE ANY POINTY-HAIRED IDIOTS RUNNING YOUR PLACE?
WOULD YOU LIKE ONE?

AS YOU REQUESTED, I BENCHMARKED OUR COMPANY AGAINST FIVE WORLD-CLASS COMPANIES.
S. Adams
THE COMPARISONS ARE IRRELEVANT BECAUSE WE'RE IN DIFFERENT INDUSTRIES. BUT THAT DIDN'T STOP ME.
6/28 © 1995 United Feature Syndicate, Inc. (NYC)
WHY CAN THEY MAKE A POTATO CHIP IN ONE SECOND BUT IT TAKES US MONTHS TO DEVELOP SOFTWARE?
I THINK THEY OIL THE CHIPS.

WE'RE GOING TO FOLLOW THE ADVICE OF THE DOGBERT CONSULTING COMPANY AND FORM "BATTLIN' BUSINESS UNITS."

S. ADAMS

6/30 © 1995 United Feature Syndicate, Inc. (NYC)

I'D LIKE YOU ALL TO MEET OUR NEW CO-OP EMPLOYEE.
S. Adams
WE DON'T PAY HIM. HE WORKS FOR FREE TO GAIN VALUABLE JOB EXPERIENCE.
I'M PUTTING YOU IN CHARGE OF THE PTG PROJECT!
WOW! WHAT IS IT ?!!
PTG STANDS FOR "PAPER TOWEL GUY."
IF SOMEBODY SPILLS COFFEE IT'S YOUR JOB TO THROW YOUR BODY ON IT BEFORE IT REACHES ONE OF US.
7/2
OOPS
FIRE IN THE HOLE !!!
© 1995 United Feature Syndicate, Inc.
HOW'D I DO?
NOT SO GOOD, KID. THAT WAS TEA.

HA HA! NOW THAT THE ENGINEERS MUST CHARGE THEIR TIME TO MARKETING, WE OWN YOU!
S. Adams
I'LL JUST REPROGRAM YOUR COMPUTER THROUGH THE LAN SO ITS RADIATION WILL ALTER YOUR DNA.
7/3 © 1995 United Feature Syndicate, Inc. (NYC)
IS THAT POSSIBLE??!
AS FAR AS YOU KNOW.
I TOLD A GUY IN MARKETING THAT I PROGRAMMED HIS COMPUTER TO ALTER HIS DNA STRUCTURE.
HEE HEE
S. Adams
HE THINKS HE'LL TURN INTO SOME KIND OF ANIMAL.
TELL HIM YOU SET IT TO "WEASEL." IT'LL TAKE LONGER TO NOTICE ANY CHANGE.
7/4 © 1995 United Feature Syndicate, Inc. (NYC)
TELL ME THE TRUTH, ALICE. CAN DILBERT REPROGRAM MY DNA?
YEAH. YOU MARKETING GUYS ONLY HAVE ONE HELIX.

MAYBE YOU SHOULDN'T HAVE TOLD STAN YOU REPROGRAMMED HIS DNA THROUGH THE LAN.
S. Adams
THOSE MARKETING GUYS BELIEVE ANYTHING. THEY EVEN BELIEVE MARKET RESEARCH, FOR HEAVEN'S SAKE.
7/5 © 1995 United Feature Syndicate, Inc. (NYC)
THERE'S NO TELLING WHAT THE POWER OF SUGGESTION MIGHT DO.
WELL, THANK YOU VERY MUCH.

I JOKINGLY TOLD STAN IN MARKETING THAT I REPROGRAMMED HIS DNA. HE'S SO GULLIBLE THAT HE'S ACTUALLY CHANGING!
S. Adams
YOU MUST USE HIS GULLIBILITY TO REVERSE THE PROCESS. REMEMBER, HIS ENTIRE REALITY IS SHAPED BY UNVERIFIED CUSTOMER ANECDOTES.
7/6 © 1995 United Feature Syndicate, Inc. (NYC)
I HEARD A RUMOR OF A STORY OF AN ALLEGED FOCUS GROUP WHERE A QUOTE TAKEN OUT OF CONTEXT INDICATES YOU'RE NOT BECOMING A WEASEL.
I'M NOT?!
YIPEEE!

OUR NEW DRESS POLICY AT WORK ALLOWS CASUAL CLOTHES ON FRIDAYS.
S. Adams
THAT'S GOOD, BECAUSE STUDIES HAVE SHOWN THAT FRIDAYS ARE THE ONLY SAFE DAY TO DRESS CASUALLY; ANY OTHER DAY WOULD CAUSE A STOCK PLUNGE.
7/7 © 1995 United Feature Syndicate, Inc. (NYC)
IS IT JUST ME OR IS THAT POLICY STUPID?
THAT'S NOT AN "OR" QUESTION.

I WANT US TO HAVE THE SAME KIND OF TEAMWORK AS THE EGYPTIANS WHO BUILT THE PYRAMIDS!
S. Adams
SOME SCHOLARS BELIEVE THE PYRAMIDS WERE BUILT BY SLAVES.
7/8 © 1995 United Feature Syndicate, Inc. (NYC)
BUT THERE'S SOME DOUBT; THAT'S ALL I'M SHOOTING FOR.
I THINK THEY WERE GUIDED BY UFOs TOO.

WE DESPERATELY NEED ANOTHER PERSON ON MY PROJECT!
WE'RE ALREADY OVER HEADCOUNT. GET A CONTRACT EMPLOYEE.
OKAY, BUT THEY COST TWICE AS MUCH.
S. Adams
PLUS WE NEED TO BUY A COMPUTER.
RENT ONE. WE'RE OVER OUR CAPITAL BUDGET.
RENTING IS EXPENSIVE. WE'LL GO OVER OUR EXPENSE BUDGET.
I'LL FIRE WALLY. THAT WILL FREE UP SOME CASH.
WALLY'S ON MY PROJECT!
7/9
FORGET IT! I'LL JUST WORK SIXTEEN HOURS A DAY!!
THAT WORKED OUT PERFECTLY. I THINK I MIGHT BE A GENIUS OR SOMETHING.
© 1995 United Feature Syndicate, Inc.
I WONDER IF I SHOULD HAVE TOLD HIM THE PROJECT WAS CANCELLED LAST WEEK.

EVERYBODY IN ENGINEERING USES THIS PROGRAM I WROTE. I THINK MARKETING SHOULD TURN IT INTO A PRODUCT.
I WOULDN'T BUY THIS.
S. Adams
THAT'S IRRELEVANT BECAUSE THE TARGET MARKET WOULD BE ENGINEERS.
ENGINEERS THINK THE SAME AS MARKETEERS.
7/10 © 1995 United Feature Syndicate, Inc. (NYC)
IF THAT WERE TRUE WE'D BE SITTING IN A CAVE TRYING TO DECIDE IF ROCKS ARE EDIBLE.
YOU KNOW, YOU COULD KEEP RECIPES ON THIS.
I AM SAINT DOGBERT. I HAVE COME TO DRIVE OUT THE STALE AND OVERUSED JOKES ABOUT THE INFORMATION SUPERHIGHWAY.
S. Adams
SOMETIMES I FEEL LIKE ROADKILL ON THE INFORMATION SUPERHIGHWAY!
7/11 © 1995 United Feature Syndicate, Inc. (NYC)
DON'T MAKE ME COME OVER THERE!
I THINK YOU LIKE THAT COMPUTER MORE THAN YOU LIKE ME.
S. Adams
THAT'S NOT TRUE, LIZ. I DO NOT LIKE THAT COMPUTER MORE THAN I LIKE YOU.
7/12 © 1995 United Feature Syndicate, Inc. (NYC)
PLEASE, PLEASE DON'T ASK ABOUT THE LAPTOP.
"THAT" COMPUTER?

OKAY, LET'S START BY DOCUMENTING YOUR MARKET REQUIREMENTS.
NO, LET'S START BY YOU TELLING ME ALL THE THINGS YOU CAN DESIGN. THEN I'LL TELL YOU WHICH ONE I LIKE.
S. Adams
7/3 © 1995 United Feature Syndicate, Inc. (NYC)
WORK CAN BE VERY REWARDING. YOU SHOULD TRY IT.
WHAT'S THAT DOOHICKEY YOU HAVE THERE?
CAROL, THE NEXT TIME YOU ORDER MY BUSINESS CARDS, SPELL OUT MY FULL TITLE: "DIRECTOR OF PRODUCT ENHANCEMENTS."
DON'T USE THE ACRONYM "DOPE."
S. Adams
7/14 © 1995 United Feature Syndicate, Inc. (NYC)
I DIDN'T KNOW YOU WERE THE DIRECTOR OF PRODUCT ENHANCE-MENTS.
I WANT YOU TO STUDY OUR OPTIONS FOR PROJECT "ZEBRA" AND MAKE A RECOMMENDATION.
TRANSLATION: "READ MY MIND THEN RECOMMEND THE OPTION I'VE ALREADY DECIDED ON."
S. Adams
7/15 © 1995 United Feature Syndicate, Inc. (NYC)
I'LL GET RIGHT ON IT!
TRANSLATION: "I AM DOOMED. I WILL GO LOOK FOR NAUGHTY PICTURES ON THE INTERNET INSTEAD."

I'VE DECIDED TO MAKE SOME CHANGES TO OUR CORPORATE CULTURE.
S.Adams
LET ME GUESS WHAT THAT MEANS.
WE'LL WORK LONGER HOURS WITHOUT EXTRA PAY...
YOUR MANAGEMENT STYLE WILL REMAIN EXACTLY THE SAME BECAUSE LORD KNOWS THERE'S NO NEED FOR YOU TO CHANGE.
WE'LL START CALLING OURSELVES A "TEAM" SO IT DOESN'T SEEM LIKE WORK!
7-16
I PREDICT THERE WILL BE VAPID SLOGANS PRINTED ON NOTEPADS, AND MAYBE SOME USELESS MEETINGS.
SHE'S PSYCHIC!
IS IT JUST ME OR IS THE CULTURE ALREADY CHANGING?
I FEEL IT! WE'RE CHANGING!
© 1995 United Feature Syndicate, Inc.
WHAT'S NEXT ON THE FAD MENU?
I WONDER IF IT'S TOO LATE TO RULE BY FEAR.

WHAT DID YOU BRING TO READ?
IT'S A BOOK OF TIPS FOR MY NEW COMPUTER GOLF GAME.
S. Adams
SO... YOU'RE READING A BOOK... ABOUT A COMPUTER SIMULATION... OF AN ACTIVITY THAT'S ALMOST A SPORT...
7/17 © 1995 United Feature Syndicate, Inc. (NYC)
THAT'S ABOUT AS CLOSE AS YOU CAN GET TO BEING A NON-ORGANIC LIFE FORM.
THIS CHAPTER IS ABOUT DRIVING THE LITTLE CART.
THAT'S AN INTERESTING SUGGESTION, WALLY. BUT IF IT'S A GOOD IDEA, WHY AREN'T OTHER COMPANIES DOING IT?
S. Adams
CAN YOU IMAGINE IN YOUR WILDEST DREAMS THAT MAYBE, JUST MAYBE I HAD A GOOD IDEA THAT NOBODY ELSE THOUGHT OF?!!
7/18 © 1995 United Feature Syndicate, Inc. (NYC)
YOU MUST HAVE SEEN IT IN A BOOK.
THANKS FOR THE CONFIDENCE IN MY ABILITIES.
YOU READ A BOOK?

I DON'T KNOW WHAT KIND OF GIFT TO BUY FOR TED'S BABY SHOWER.
S. Adams
HAND-CRAFTED ITEMS ARE GOOD. CUT THREE HOLES IN A PAPER BAG AND YOU'VE GOT A LOVELY BABY DRESS.
7/19 © 1995 United Feature Syndicate, Inc. (NYC)
HE MIGHT THINK I'M CHEAP.
DO YOU THINK THE KID HAS A SALT SHAKER YET?

TED'S BABY SHOWER
OH LOOK, IT'S A STAPLER...
S. Adams
I CAN USE THIS TO TAKE UP THE HEM ON THE LOVELY HAND-CRAFTED PAPER BAG DRESS THAT DILBERT MADE.
7/20 © 1995 United Feature Syndicate, Inc. (NYC)
IT LOOKS JUST LIKE THE ONE THAT DISAPPEARED FROM MY CUBICLE THIS MORNING.
EXCEPT YOURS HAD STAPLES.
IT'S REALLY DIFFERENT AROUND HERE SINCE WE LOST DILBERT'S DAD.
WHEN DID HE DIE?
S. Adams
HE'S NOT DEAD. WE LOST HIM AT THE MALL, CHRISTMAS OF '92.
7/21 © 1995 United Feature Syndicate, Inc. (NYC)
SHOULDN'T YOU BE LOOKING FOR HIM?
I SAID IT'S DIFFERENT, NOT WORSE.
I CAN'T BELIEVE YOUR FATHER HAS BEEN LOST AT THE MALL SINCE 1992!
S. Adams
IF MY FATHER OR MY HUSBAND WERE LOST AT THE MALL I'D BE SEARCHING FOR HIM TWENTY-FOUR HOURS A DAY!!
7/22 © 1995 United Feature Syndicate, Inc. (NYC)
WE'RE WAITING FOR A SALE.
YOU'RE A BIT OF A WHINER, AREN'T YOU, DEAR?

I HAD A FEW SUGGESTIONS ON YOUR DOCUMENT, ALICE.
S.Adams
THANKS
BONK
I'VE MADE SOME UPGRADES TO YOUR DOCUMENT, ALICE.
THAT'S JUST WHAT IT NEEDED: A BUNCH OF OBTUSE ACRONYMS AND JARGON.
OOOH, LOOKY! YOU'VE ALSO MADE ELEGANT MULTI-TOPIC SENTENCES OUT OF MY STUBBY CLEAR ONES!
7/23
THANK YOU. AND PUT ME DOWN AS THE AUTHOR SINCE I'M THE BOSS.
MAYBE I SHOULD DISTRIBUTE LITTLE PLASTIC STATUES OF YOU WITH EVERY COPY. HOW ABOUT THAT?
© 1995 United Feature Syndicate, Inc.
HERE'S YOUR COPY, HERE'S YOUR STATUE, DON'T ASK.
OUR QUALITY IS LOW, BUT AT LEAST WE DON'T GET CREDIT.

AS USUAL, THE BOSS IS LATE. WHAT DO YOU WANT TO DO?
LET'S PRACTICE MAKING SMALL TALK. IT'LL COME IN HANDY WHEN WE MEET WITH MARKETING.
SO, ALICE, HAVEN'T WE SEEN THAT OUTFIT A LOT?
THIS CHAIR IS SPRINGY. DO YOU THINK THEY'RE ALL SPRINGY?
S. Adams
7/24 © 1995 United Feature Syndicate, Inc. (NYC)

IT'S AMAZING HOW MUCH WE'VE CHANGED SINCE PREHISTORIC TIMES.
OUR ANCESTORS JUST SAT AROUND IN CAVES, GRUNTING AND DRAWING ON THE WALL.
NOT VERY PRODUCTIVE.
IT WAS JUST THIS, ALL DAY LONG.
MMM. YUP.
S. Adams
7/25 © 1995 United Feature Syndicate, Inc. (NYC)

MY PROPOSED WORK PLAN FOR THE YEAR IS TO STRESS-TEST OUR PRODUCT UNDER SEVERE NETWORK CONDITIONS.
I WILL ACCOMPLISH THIS BY DOWNLOADING LARGE IMAGE FILES FROM THE BUSIEST SERVERS ON THE NET.
I WAS THIS CLOSE TO MAKING IT MY JOB TO DOWNLOAD NAUGHTY PICTURES.
IT'S JUST AS WELL; I WOULD HAVE HAD TO KILL YOU.
S. Adams
7/26 © 1995 United Feature Syndicate, Inc. (NYC)

BOB, YOUR SELF-ESTEEM MIGHT IMPROVE IF YOU GOT A JOB.
AS WHAT?
S. Adams
THERE'S AN OPENING IN OUR PROCUREMENT DEPARTMENT. YOU'D BE PERFECT.
WHAT DOES PROCUREMENT DO?
7/27 © 1995 United Feature Syndicate, Inc. (NYC)
THEIR JOB IS TO PREVENT US FROM GETTING THE COMPUTERS WE WANT.
CAN I HIT PEOPLE WITH MY TAIL?

BOB WORKS IN PROCUREMENT
YOUR DUTIES ARE SIMPLE. PEOPLE WILL COME TO YOU AND ASK FOR THINGS.
S. Adams
ASSUME ALL EMPLOYEES ARE LYING, TREASURE-HUNTING THIEVES. GIVE THEM LOW-COST SUBSTITUTES AND CLAIM THE SAVINGS ON YOUR ACCOMPLISHMENTS.
7/28 © 1995 United Feature Syndicate, Inc. (NYC)
I ASKED FOR A MULTIMEDIA LAPTOP PC. THIS IS A "DYMO" LABELER.
NICE TRY, PAUL, IF THAT'S YOUR REAL NAME.

BOB IN PROCUREMENT
I'M AFRAID THE EQUIPMENT YOU WANT IS NOT ON THE APPROVED EQUIPMENT LIST.
S. Adams
LET ME THINK... IF I ADD THIS TO THE APPROVED LIST, THAT'S MORE WORK FOR ME... BUT IF I SAY NO, IT'S MORE WORK FOR YOU... HMM...THINK, THINK...
7/29 © 1995 United Feature Syndicate, Inc. (NYC)
I'D LIKE TO SEE THIS ALLEGED LIST.
WELL, IT'S NOT SO MUCH A PHYSICAL LIST AS IT IS A PHILOSOPHY.

OUR NEW VP SAYS HE HAS AN "OPEN DOOR POLICY." LET'S CHECK IT OUT.
S. ADAMS
KNOCK KNOCK
HI HO. NOTHING IMPORTANT. WE JUST WANTED TO DROP IN.
THIS OPEN DOOR POLICY IS GREAT. OUR LAST VP WAS ALOOF.
ARE THOSE SOURBALLS?
LOOK AT ALL THE FURNITURE IN HERE!
I CALL COUCH!
IS THERE SOMETHING I CAN DO FOR YOU?
WELL... SOMETIMES OUR CUBICLES ARE TOO HOT.
COULD YOU HAVE SOMEBODY LOOK INTO IT?
7-30 © 1995 United Feature Syndicate, Inc.
BOY, THOSE SOURBALLS SURE LULL YOU INTO A FALSE SENSE OF SECURITY.
THE MAN IS LIKE A HUGE INSINCERE SPIDER.

I THINK, THEREFORE I AM.
BUT I'M MICROMANAGED, THEREFORE I AM NOT.
S. Adams
7/31 © 1995 United Feature Syndicate, Inc. (NYC)
I HAVE A PHILOSOPHICAL QUESTION FOR YOU.
YOU'RE NOT ME, THEREFORE YOU'RE IRRELEVANT.
WE'RE PLANNING TO HIRE A TEMP AT WORK. YOU SHOULD APPLY FOR THE JOB, RATBERT.
WOW! ME? A TEMP?!
S. Adams
AS A TEMP I WOULD FINALLY GET ALL OF THE RESPECT AND UNCONDITIONAL LOVE THAT I DESERVE!!
8/1 © 1995 United Feature Syndicate, Inc. (NYC)
DANGER: SHARP LEARNING CURVE AHEAD.
I ASSUME I'LL GET AN OFFICE AND A SECRETARY.

I SUBMIT MYSELF AS A CANDIDATE FOR THE POSITION OF "TEMPORARY EMPLOYEE."
S. Adams
I'M VERY TEMPORARY. FIRST I'LL BE IN ONE PLACE AND THEN YOU BLINK AND I'M GONE! BLINK, GONE, BLINK, GONE, BLINK, GONE...
8/2 © 1995 United Feature Syndicate, Inc. (NYC)
STOP SAYING "BLINK, GONE." IT'S MAKING ME NUTS.
IT APPEARS THAT THE BALANCE OF POWER HAS SHIFTED MY WAY.

CONGRATULATIONS ON GETTING HIRED AS A TEMP, RATBERT.
WHERE DO I START?!
S. Adams
YOUR OFFICE IS THIS CARDBOARD BOX IN THE MAIN HALLWAY. THE REGULAR EMPLOYEES WILL NOT MAKE EYE CONTACT OR ASK YOUR NAME.
8/3 © 1995 United Feature Syndicate, Inc. (NYC)
YOUR STATUS IS ROUGHLY BETWEEN THE SECURITY GUARD AND THE CRUD BEHIND THE REFRIGERATOR.
DO I GET A COMPANY CAR?

RATBERT THE TEMP WORKER
THIS IS REALLY TESTING MY SENSE OF SELF-WORTH.
S. Adams
I WILL COMPENSATE BY SHOUTING A LIST OF MY TALENTS TO ANYBODY WHO WALKS PAST.
8/4 © 1995 United Feature Syndicate, Inc. (NYC)
IGNORE HIM. HE'S TRYING TO TRICK US INTO MAKING EYE CONTACT.
I EAT RUBBER! I CARRY DISEASE! I ENJOY OPERA!

RATBERT THE TEMP WORKER
I'M ONLY A TEMP, BUT I DEMAND RESPECT!!
S. Adams
OKAY, MAYBE THAT'S TOO MUCH TO ASK. BUT I DEMAND THAT SOMEBODY MAKE EYE CONTACT WITH ME!!
8/5 © 1995 United Feature Syndicate, Inc. (NYC)
HOW'S THIS?
THAT'S PERIPHERAL VISION!!!

WHEN DID YOU START BELIEVING THAT YOUR BOSS WAS AN EVIL ENTITY FROM ANOTHER DIMENSION?
S.Adams
I'D LIKE TO SIT IN ON YOUR CUSTOMER MEETING.
UH-OH
LET ME SHARE THE HIGH LEVEL STRATEGIC VIEW.
HERE WE GO.
LIFE BEGAN IN THE PRIMORDIAL STEW LITERALLY HUNDREDS OF YEARS AGO...
BUT WE ARE THE ONLY COMPANY WHO EVER FOUND SYNERGIES IN OUR WIN-WIN SOLUTIONS!
© 1996 United Feature Syndicate, Inc. (NYC)
8/6
TWO HOURS LATER
AND WE WON'T STOP UNTIL WE DELIGHT EVERY CUSTOMER!
I'D BE DELIGHTED IF YOU JUST TOLD ME ABOUT YOUR NEW INTERNET ACCESS PRODUCT.
I CANCELLED THE FUNDING YESTER-DAY.
WHO'S UP FOR A TOUR OF OUR CUBICLES?
GOTTA GO.

CATBERT THE HR DIRECTOR
I THINK I'LL INVENT SOME ILLOGICAL POLICIES TO ANNOY EMPLOYEES.
MY DIABOLICAL NEW DRESS CODE WILL MAKE THEM QUESTION THEIR OWN SANITY.
S.Adams
8/7 © 1995 United Feature Syndicate, Inc. (NYC)
... SO, CASUAL CLOTHES DON'T LOWER OUR STOCK VALUE... BUT ONLY IF WORN ON FRIDAYS... UNLESS SOMEBODY SEES US... GOT IT?
I THINK I'M INSANE.

I DON'T UNDERSTAND YOUR NEW DRESS CODE POLICY, MR. CATBERT.
MAYBE YOU'RE INSANE.
S.Adams
IT'S SIMPLE. FRIDAYS ARE "CASUAL." BUT YOU CAN'T WEAR JEANS BECAUSE JEANS LOOK GOOD AND FEEL GOOD AND YOU ALREADY OWN SEVERAL PAIRS.
8/8 © 1995 United Feature Syndicate, Inc. (NYC)
IT'S ANOTHER SADISTIC HUMAN RESOURCES PLOT TO MAKE PEOPLE QUIT!!
SAY HELLO TO UNSIGHTLY PANTY LINES.

WELL, IT WOULDN'T BE FRIDAY IF I DIDN'T SEE ALICE WEARING HER ONE PAIR OF TAN PANTS.
S.Adams
I LOVE THE "BUSINESS CASUAL" LOOK FOR THE WAY IT COMBINES UNATTRACTIVE WITH UNPROFESSIONAL WHILE DIMINISHING NEITHER.
8/9 © 1995 United Feature Syndicate, Inc. (NYC)
DO YOU THINK THE FASHION OPINION OF A MALE ENGINEER MATTERS TO ME??
TWINS!

MY PLAN IS TO MAKE YOU A SELF-DIRECTED TEAM.
AFTER A FEW TEAM MEETINGS, THE DISRESPECT YOU HAVE FOR EACH OTHER WILL FESTER AND GROW INTO FULL-BLOWN LOATHING.
YOU'LL BEG ME TO MICRO-MANAGE YOU!! HA HA HA!!
IT ACTUALLY FEELS GOOD TO HAVE A PLAN.
S. Adams
8/10 © 1995 United Feature Syndicate, Inc. (NYC)

I'M REORGANIZING THE DEPARTMENT INTO FAST-MOVING TEAMS.
GOOD PLAN. WE'LL NEVER REALIZE WE'RE POWERLESS, MICRO-MANAGED SERFS AFTER WE CALL OURSELVES A "TEAM."
I NEED SOME LESS EXPERI-ENCED PEOPLE.
I FEEL FASTER ALREADY.
THE G-FORCES ARE KILLING ME.
S. Adams
8/11 © 1995 United Feature Syndicate, Inc. (NYC)

AS YOU REQUESTED, I DROPPED EVERYTHING AND WROTE MY CAREER DEVELOPMENT PLAN.
I PLAN TO BOUNCE FROM ONE ARTIFICIAL EMERGEN-CY TO ANOTHER, LIKE A PING-PONG BALL IN A CLOTHES DRYER, UNTIL ONE DAY I RESIGN.
HERE I'M USING HUMOR TO MAKE A POINT...
FAX THIS TO HR NOW!!
S. Adams
8/12 © 1995 United Feature Syndicate, Inc. (NYC)

HERE'S HOW YOUR MARKETING DEPARTMENT CAN HELP RETAIN YOUR BEST ENGINEERS.
MARKETING GETS AN IDEA
WE'LL LEVERAGE OUR TECHNOLOGY BY BUILDING ANT FARMS.
SPREADSHEETS MAKE THE IDEA LOOK PROFITABLE.
THE ANT MILK ALONE WILL BE A POSITIVE NPV!
WOW!
WHAT'S AN NPV?
DON'T FORGET THE "WORST CASE SCENARIO."
WORST CASE, SOMEBODY BUILDS A GIGANTIC MAGNIFYING GLASS NEXT DOOR...
SOLUTION: BITE-SIZED ANT JERKY!
THERE'S NO RISK!
AN ENGINEER WILL BE ASSIGNED TO THE PROJECT.
ANT FARMS! DO IT!
UH-OH.
THE ENGINEER WILL CHALLENGE THE ASSUMPTIONS
YOU CAN'T GET A GALLON OF MILK FROM AN ANT!
WHAT DO YOU KNOW ABOUT MARKETING?
RESULT: THE ENGINEER WILL NEVER LEAVE THE COMPANY.
SO... YOUR CURRENT JOB IS "ANT FARM ENGINEER"?
I'M DOOMED.
S Adams
© 1995 United Feature Syndicate, Inc. (NYC)
8/13

MY STATUS FOR THE WEEK IS THAT THE ONGOING DEHUMANIZATION FROM MY JOB HAS CAUSED ME TO DOUBT MY EXISTENCE.
THERE IS REASON TO BELIEVE I AM BECOMING INVISIBLE.
DO I HEAR YOUR PAGER BUZZING, WALLY?
I DOUBT IT; I DON'T KEEP BATTERIES IN IT.
PLINK
S. Adams
8/14 © 1995 United Feature Syndicate, Inc. (NYC)

THE DEHUMANIZATION OF MY JOB HAS RENDERED ME INVISIBLE TO HUMANS. ONLY YOU CAN SEE ME, DOGBERT.
HOW CAN WE FIX THIS?
YOU COULD WEAR A BAG ON YOUR HEAD WHEN YOU'RE AROUND ME.
THAT'S NOT THE FIX I HAD IN MIND.
IT'S NOT A PERFECT SOLUTION. I'D STILL BE ABLE TO HEAR YOU.
S. Adams
8/15 © 1995 United Feature Syndicate, Inc. (NYC)

YOU'RE INVISIBLE TO YOUR CO-WORKERS. BUT YOU CAN COMPENSATE BY FORMING A SYMBIOTIC RELATIONSHIP WITH A VISIBLE CREATURE.
RATBERT WILL CLING TO YOUR BACK. HE'LL BE YOUR VISUAL AND AUDITORY LINK WITH YOUR CO-WORKERS.
SO... WORKING HARD? OR HARDLY WORKING?
I KNEW THIS COLOMBIAN COFFEE WAS TROUBLE.
S. Adams
8/16 © 1995 United Feature Syndicate, Inc. (NYC)

DON'T BE ALARMED. I'M NOT REALLY A RAT FLOATING IN MIDAIR.
S. Adams
I'M CLINGING TO THE BACK OF AN EMPLOYEE WHO HAS BEEN RENDERED INVISIBLE BY A LONG SUCCESSION OF WORTHLESS ASSIGNMENTS.
8/17 © 1995 United Feature Syndicate, Inc. (NYC)
LOOKS LIKE AN ISOLATED CASE OF BAD ATTITUDE.
WHICH ROOM IS THE "QUALITY" MEETING IN?
I SIGNIFICANTLY INCREASED MY VISIBILITY AT WORK TODAY, DOGBERT.
S. Adams
YESTERDAY I WAS INVISIBLE TO MY MANAGEMENT. BUT TODAY I AM KNOWN BY ALL.
8/18 © 1995 United Feature Syndicate, Inc. (NYC)
YOU SCREWED UP, HUH?
OOH YEAH. BIG TIME.
I KNOW WHERE YOU'RE GOING.
S. Adams
YOU'RE GOING TO A MEETING WHERE EQUALLY UNINFORMED MANAGERS WILL MAKE DECISIONS THAT NEUTER THE WORK I DID ALL WEEK.
8/19 © 1995 United Feature Syndicate, Inc. (NYC)
YOU DIDN'T DO ANY WORK THIS WEEK.
I THINK I'VE GOT THIS WHOLE "WORK" CONCEPT FIGURED OUT.

PLEASE DON'T PROMISE THE PRODUCT MANAGER MORE THAN WE CAN DELIVER.
S. Adams
WE NEED A TOTALLY NEW SOFTWARE INTERFACE IN ONE MONTH.
YOU GOT IT!
AND REWRITE THE OPERATING SYSTEM SO WE DOMINATE THE INDUSTRY.
CONCURRENT DEVELOPMENT.
CHECK
SUDDENLY I FEEL OMNIPOTENT.
I WANT ALL NEW HARDWARE, ANTI-GRAVITY PACKAGING, HOLOGRAPHIC AGENTS...
YAWN YAWN
© 1995 United Feature Syndicate, Inc. (NYC)
8/20
CAN YOUR TEAM REALLY DO THAT IN A MONTH?
LET ME GET THEIR REACTION.
AAAGH!!
PESSIMISM WILL NOT LOOK GOOD ON YOUR PERFORMANCE REVIEW.
TWITCH

YOUR EXPENSE REPORT WAS REJECTED BY ACCOUNTING.
WHY?
S. Adams
BECAUSE THE EMPTINESS OF THEIR SHALLOW LIVES MAKES THEM WANT TO HURT OTHERS IN ORDER TO VALIDATE THEIR PATHETIC EXISTENCE.
8/21 © 1995 United Feature Syndicate, Inc. (NYC)
CAN YOU HELP ME CLEAR THIS UP?
TO BE HONEST, I'M KINDA BUYING IN TO THEIR PHILOSOPHY.
IF IT'S OKAY, I'LL HOLD ONTO MY SOUL WHILE I VISIT THE ACCOUNTING DEPARTMENT.
SOUL CHECK
TIPS
S. Adams
I CAME TO ANSWER YOUR QUESTIONS ABOUT MY EXPENSE REPORT.
TAKE A SEAT.
8/22 © 1995 United Feature Syndicate, Inc. (NYC)
I DON'T LIKE THE WAY THIS IS STARTING.

DILBERT'S EXPENSE VOUCHER
WHAT ARE YOU TRYING TO PULL?? DO YOU THINK WE'RE IDIOTS IN ACCOUNTING?!!
S. Adams
NO, I SWEAR, I THINK YOU'RE SMART BUT SADISTIC TROLLS WITH MANY HUMANOID CHARACTERISTICS.
8/23 © 1995 United Feature Syndicate, Inc. (NYC)
APPARENTLY THERE WAS NO RIGHT ANSWER.

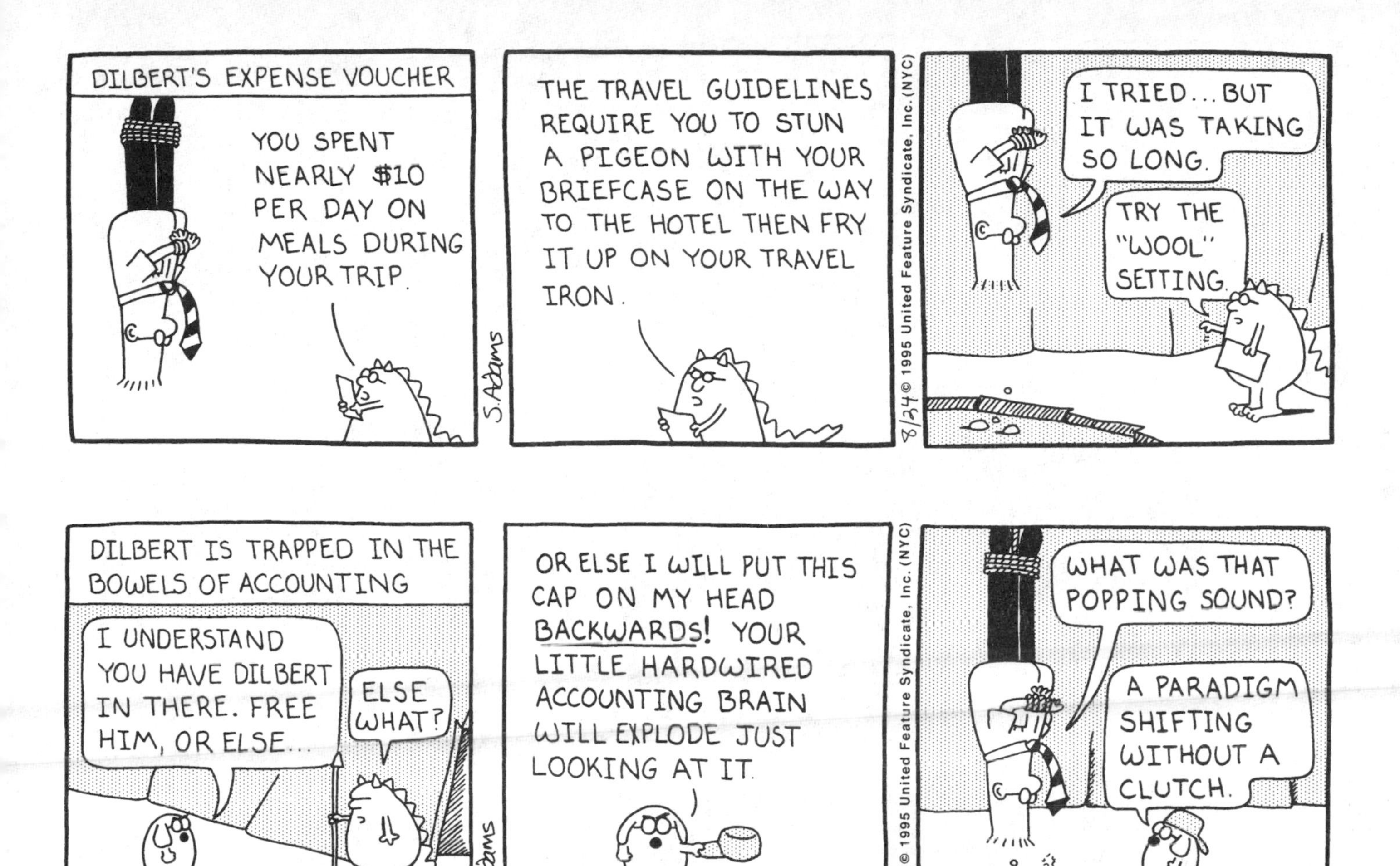
DILBERT'S EXPENSE VOUCHER
YOU SPENT NEARLY $10 PER DAY ON MEALS DURING YOUR TRIP.
S. Adams
THE TRAVEL GUIDELINES REQUIRE YOU TO STUN A PIGEON WITH YOUR BRIEFCASE ON THE WAY TO THE HOTEL THEN FRY IT UP ON YOUR TRAVEL IRON.
8/24 © 1995 United Feature Syndicate, Inc. (NYC)
I TRIED... BUT IT WAS TAKING SO LONG.
TRY THE "WOOL" SETTING.
DILBERT IS TRAPPED IN THE BOWELS OF ACCOUNTING
I UNDERSTAND YOU HAVE DILBERT IN THERE. FREE HIM, OR ELSE...
ELSE WHAT?
S. Adams
OR ELSE I WILL PUT THIS CAP ON MY HEAD BACKWARDS! YOUR LITTLE HARDWIRED ACCOUNTING BRAIN WILL EXPLODE JUST LOOKING AT IT.
8/25 © 1995 United Feature Syndicate, Inc. (NYC)
WHAT WAS THAT POPPING SOUND?
A PARADIGM SHIFTING WITHOUT A CLUTCH.

SOMETIMES I FEEL SELF-CONSCIOUS BECAUSE MY BRAIN IS SO TINY.
S. Adams
HERE, LET ME REACH IN MY EAR AND PULL IT OUT.
8/26 © 1995 United Feature Syndicate, Inc. (NYC)
I THINK THAT'S EAR WAX, BOB.
MAYBE. BUT I'M PUTTING IT BACK JUST IN CASE.

I MADE A FEW CHANGES TO THE DESIGN.
WE'LL HAVE TO WORK AROUND THE CLOCK FOR MONTHS TO MAKE THESE CHANGES!!
S. Adams
WORK SMARTER, NOT HARDER.
YOU'RE TRYING TO VIOLATE THE LAWS OF PHYSICS!
RULES WERE MADE TO BE BROKEN.
© 1995 United Feature Syndicate, Inc. (NYC)
8/27
THIS DESIGN WOULD CREATE ENOUGH RADIATION TO INSTANTLY KILL THE USER!!
BE SURE TO MENTION THAT IN THE DOCU- MENTATION.
LET'S WORK SMARTER NOT HARDER.
I THINK WE FOUND THE ONLY "BETA" TESTER WE'LL NEED.

TINA, YOU'LL HAVE TO HAVE ALL THE DOCUMENTATION WRITTEN BY NEXT WEEK SO WE CAN SHIP IT WHEN THE SOFTWARE IS DONE.
S. Adams
HOW CAN I WRITE INSTRUCTIONS FOR SOMETHING THAT DOESN'T EXIST YET?
YOU'LL HAVE TO MAKE LOGICAL GUESSES.
8/28 © 1995 United Feature Syndicate, Inc.(NYC)
"IF YOU PRESS ANY KEY YOUR COMPUTER WILL LOCK UP. IF YOU CALL OUR TECH SUPPORT WE'LL BLAME 'MICROSOFT.'"

I FEEL LIKE TWEAKING SOME BRITTLE PEOPLE. DO YOU KNOW ANY BRITTLE PEOPLE?
S. Adams
TRY TINA THE TECH WRITER. SHE BELIEVES THAT ALL FORMS OF EXPRESSION ARE AN INSULT TO HER GENDER AND HER PROFESSION.
8/29 © 1995 United Feature Syndicate, Inc.(NYC)
THE STATUE OF "VENUS DE MILO" HAS NO ARMS.
OH, I GET IT. YOU'RE SAYING THAT WOMEN CAN'T LIFT HEAVY OBJECTS.

DOGBERT TWEAKS TINA THE BRITTLE TECH WRITER.
WHAT DO YOU THINK OF THE MOVIE "THELMA AND LOUISE"?
S. Adams
I KNOW WHAT YOU'RE TRYING TO SAY. YOU THINK ALL WOMEN ARE BAD DRIVERS. THAT'S REALLY THE POINT OF THE MOVIE, ISN'T IT??
8/30 © 1995 United Feature Syndicate, Inc.(NYC)
IF YOU'RE NOT OFFENDED YET, TUNE IN TOMORROW.
THE "THREE STOOGES"?
WHY ARE ALL OF THE DOCUMENTARIES ABOUT MEN??!

DOGBERT TWEAKS TINA THE BRITTLE TECH WRITER
IS TECHNICAL WRITING THE SAME AS WORD PROCESSING?
NO!!!
S. Adams
I AM A HIGHLY SKILLED COMMUNICATIONS PROFESSIONAL! I CAN TAKE JUMBLES OF INERT THOUGHTS AND BRING THEM TO LIFE!!
8/31 © 1995 United Feature Syndicate, Inc.(NYC)
MY SECRETARY IS RUNNING THE STAFF MEETING. I NEED YOU TO RETYPE THIS ORG CHART.
THE DOCTOR IS IN!
THIS WEEK WE INTRODUCED TINA THE BRITTLE TECH WRITER TO THE STRIP. TINA IS DYSFUNCTIONAL LIKE EVERYBODY HERE EXCEPT ME.
RRRR
S. Adams
SEND YOUR OPINIONS BY E-MAIL TO SCOTTADAMS@AOL.COM
IT'S THE ONLY WAY WE CAN LEARN.
RRRR
9/1 © 1995 United Feature Syndicate, Inc.(NYC)
PICK ONE
A. WOMEN SHOULD ONLY BE PORTRAYED AS LAWYERS AND STARSHIP CAPTAINS.
B. I DON'T HAVE E-MAIL.
C. TINA SHOULD BE TREATED WITH THE SAME DIGNITY AS DILBERT AND WALLY.
D. TAKE AN ART CLASS.

RECORDS RETENTION
S. Adams
THESE VALUABLE DOCUMENTS SHOULD BE STORED FOR FIVE YEARS.
9/2 © 1995 United Feature Syndicate, Inc.(NYC)
THIS JOB GOT SO MUCH EASIER WHEN I REALIZED THAT NOBODY EVER ASKS FOR ANYTHING BACK.

MY LAPTOP PC KEEPS FREEZING UP. COME TAKE A LOOK AT IT.
I'M TELECOMMUTING, DOGBERT. I CAN'T BE DISTRACTED BY HOME PROJECTS.
S. Adams
DON'T COME ANOTHER STEP CLOSER. THIS IS MY VIRTUAL CUBICLE, WITHIN WHICH I CAN NOT BE DISTURBED.
THESE INVISIBLE WALLS FORM A CONE OF PRODUCTIVITY AROUND ME.
WITHIN THIS ZONE I AM A DEDICATED EMPLOYEE, TOTALLY FOCUSED ON THE CORPORATE VISION.
© 1995 United Feature Syndicate, Inc.(NYC)
9/3
NOTHING CAN DISTRACT ME FROM MY FIRM COMMITMENT TO THE WORK-AT-HOME PRINCIPLE.
FINE. I THINK I'LL SET THE COUCH ON FIRE.
ANOTHER VICTORY FOR THE DISTRACTOR!
I SWEAR, SOMEDAY PRINCIPLE WILL WIN!

PROFITS ARE DOWN, MORALE IS SINKING; IT'S TIME FOR BOLD LEADERSHIP!!
S. Adams
SO I GOT SOME INSPIRATIONAL POSTERS FEATURING A VARIETY OF RELEVANT NATURE SCENES.
9/4 © 1995 United Feature Syndicate, Inc.(NYC)
I THINK YOU CAN RELATE TO THIS SCENE.
AM I THE SEAGULL OR THE CLAM?
MY NEW INSPIRATIONAL POSTER IS SO EFFECTIVE THAT I DECIDED TO CARRY IT WITH ME.
S. Adams
WHAT DO YOU THINK, ALICE? ARE YOU INSPIRED?
I'D REALLY HAVE TO SEE THE FRONT...
9/5 © 1995 United Feature Syndicate, Inc.(NYC)
HMM... I DON'T THINK THERE'S A WIN-WIN SCENARIO HERE...
TELL ME ABOUT IT...

MY INSPIRATIONAL POSTERS AREN'T WORKING. I NEED TO DO SOME ANIMAL RESEARCH, RATBERT.
READY!!
S. Adams
IN THIS BEAUTIFUL SCENE WE SEE A MIGHTY EAGLE SWOOPING DOWN TO CAPTURE ITS PREY. WHAT IS YOUR REACTION?
9/6 © 1995 United Feature Syndicate, Inc.(NYC)
I THINK IT'S WORKING.
RUN FOR IT, MOM!!!

I SHOULD QUIT AND BECOME A CONTRACT EMPLOYEE. THEN I'D HAVE MORE INCOME AND I'D FEEL THE WIND IN MY HAIR.
S. Adams
IT'S POSSIBLE YOU'D HAVE NO INCOME AT ALL...
9/7 © 1995 United Feature Syndicate, Inc.(NYC)
AND IF YOU WANT WIND IN YOUR HAIR YOU'LL HAVE TO TAKE OFF YOUR SHIRT AND RUN AROUND WITH YOUR ARMS UP.
THANK YOU FOR YOUR SUPPORT.

ALICE, I'M THINKING ABOUT QUITTING AND BECOMING A CONTRACT EMPLOYEE. DO YOU HAVE ANY ADVICE?
S. Adams
SLEEP IN DOORWAYS SO IT DOESN'T RAIN ON YOU. THE BEST SHOPPING CARTS ARE AT "LUCKY." YOU CAN MAKE AN EXCELLENT SIGN WITH A BLACK MARKING PEN AND A HUNK OF CARDBOARD.
9/8 © 1995 United Feature Syndicate, Inc.(NYC)
I HATE ALL OF MY CO-WORKERS.
DESPITE THE NAME, FOOD STAMPS ARE NOT EDIBLE.

I NEED TO THINK "OUTSIDE THE BOX" TO COME UP WITH A CREATIVE DESIGN...
S. Adams
I PUSH MY CHAIR INTO THE HALLWAY TO CHANGE MY VIEWPOINT AND STIMULATE MY CREATIVE JUICES.
9/9 © 1995 United Feature Syndicate, Inc.(NYC)
SUDDENLY MY JUICE DRIES UP.
YOU'RE A FIRE HAZARD. DO YOUR THINKING INSIDE YOUR BOX.

WE JUST HIRED JACK AWAY FROM OUR COMPETITOR. HE WAS THEIR BEST MANAGER.
S. Adams
JACK WILL BE IN CHARGE OF PROJECT "GOOSEFOOD."
I'D LIKE YOU TWO TO BRIEF JACK ON THE PROJECT.
PROJECT "GOOSEFOOD" HAS NO BUDGET AND NO MANAGEMENT SUPPORT.
YOUR JOB IS TO BUILD A GLOBAL INFORMATION NETWORK IN TWO WEEKS.
© 1995 United Feature Syndicate, Inc.(NYC)
FAILURE IS CERTAIN. SOON YOU WILL LEAVE THE INDUSTRY IN DISGRACE.
9/10
... JUST LIKE THE OTHER "BEST MANAGERS" WE HIRED FROM OUR COMPETITORS.
JUST OUT OF CURIOSITY, HOW DID THE PROJECT GET ITS NAME?
LET'S JUST SAY THAT YOU'RE THE GOOSE FOOD...

AS DIRECTOR OF HUMAN RESOURCES I'VE BEEN ASKED TO REDUCE THE COST OF EMPLOYEE BENEFITS.
S. Adams
THE COMPANY WILL NO LONGER PAY FOR EYE-GLASSES. BUT WE WILL SUPPORT A NEW VISION-CORRECTION PROCEDURE.
9/11
© 1995 United Feature Syndicate, Inc.(NYC)
RADIAL KERATOTOMY?
SQUINTING.

I HAVE TO CUT JANITOR EXPENSES. DO YOU THINK I'LL HAVE ANY HR ISSUES IF I MAKE EMPLOYEES EMPTY THEIR OWN TRASH?
S. Adams
WE'LL SOFTEN THE BAD NEWS BY SIMULTANEOUSLY INTRODUCING A NEW EMPLOYEE FITNESS PROGRAM...
9/12 © 1995 United Feature Syndicate, Inc.(NYC)
OKAY, EVERYBODY, IT'S TIME TO TRASHERCISE!!!

I'M WRITING AN E-MAIL TO PROTEST THE NEW POLICY OF MAKING THE EMPLOYEES EMPTY THEIR OWN TRASH AT NIGHT.
S. Adams
IT'S STUPID TO HAVE HIGHLY PAID ENGINEERS DOING UNPRODUCTIVE TASKS WHEN WE COULD BE INVENTING THE FUTURE!
9/13 © 1995 United Feature Syndicate, Inc.(NYC)
ARE YOU COMING TO THE "QUALITY FAIRE"?
NO, THIS WILL TAKE ANOTHER HOUR.

HERE'S THE PROBLEM. WE'VE GOT A WHOLE NEST OF PAPER TROLLS.
S. Adams
AAIIEE!
9/14 © 1995 United Feature Syndicate, Inc.(NYC)
IF I CALL 911 NOW I'LL NEVER KNOW IF THE LOWER PAPER TRAY WOULD HAVE WORKED.
HERE'S MY TIME SHEET, FILLED OUT IN INCREMENTS OF FIFTEEN MINUTES.
S. Adams
AS USUAL, I CODED THE USELESS HOURS SPENT IN MEETINGS AS "WORK," WHEREAS THE TIME I SPENT IN THE SHOWER DESIGNING CIRCUITS IN MY MIND IS "NON-WORK."
9/15 © 1995 United Feature Syndicate, Inc.(NYC)
INTERESTINGLY, EVEN THE TIME I SPEND COMPLAINING ABOUT MY LACK OF PRODUCTIVITY IS CONSIDERED "WORK."
I HATE MY LIFE.

IF THE DEPARTMENT MEETS ITS GOAL FOR THE QUARTER YOU CAN SHAVE MY HEAD!
S. Adams
THAT WOULD BE A BIG IMPROVEMENT.
HE'S TRYING TO SAVE MONEY ON A HAIRCUT
9/16 © 1995 United Feature Syndicate, Inc.(NYC)
IF WE DOUBLE OUR GOAL CAN WE IRON YOUR SHIRT, TOO?
I NEED SOME LESS EXPERIENCED EMPLOYEES.

IT'S TIME FOR MARKETING TO PUT THE GLITTER ON THIS SOFTWARE YOU'VE CREATED.
S.Adams
WITH MY GUIDANCE THIS WILL BECOME THE PREMIER DATA BACKUP SOFTWARE!
BEAR IN MIND THAT WE SAID IT WOULD TAKE SIX MONTHS TO WRITE IT.
YOU ONLY GAVE US A MONTH.
WE'LL FIX THE BUGS IN THE NEXT RELEASE.
TELL ME ABOUT THE FEATURES.
AT THIS POINT ALL IT DOES IS ERASE YOUR DISK DRIVE.
UNLESS YOU'RE ON A NETWORK.
© 1995 United Feature Syndicate, Inc.(NYC)
WHAT HAPPENS IF YOU'RE ON A NETWORK?
IT ERASES EVERYBODY'S DISK DRIVES.
9/17
AND HEAVEN HELP YOU IF YOU HAVE A MODEM...
IT CALLS ALL YOUR FRIENDS AND ERASES THEIR PCs.
WE'LL CALL IT "QuikProtect."
IF YOU HAVE A SOUND CARD IT SWEARS AT YOU.

WHERE ARE YOU TAKING ALL OF THAT OFFICE EQUIPMENT?
I'M HAVING A GARAGE SALE.
S. Adams
OUR NEW COMPANY SLOGAN IS "ACT LIKE YOU OWN THE COMPANY." SO I'VE BEEN SELLING THE STUFF THAT I DON'T USE AND KEEPING THE MONEY.
9/18 © 1995 United Feature Syndicate, Inc.(NYC)
IS THAT MY NEW COLOR MONITOR?
YEAH, I NEVER USED THAT THING.
I'M HAPPY TO REPORT THAT I HAVE EMBRACED THE NEW COMPANY SLOGAN "ACT LIKE YOU OWN THE COMPANY."
S. Adams
THIS MORNING I FIRED THE MARKETING DEPARTMENT AND HAD SECURITY ESCORT THEM OUT.
9/19 © 1995 United Feature Syndicate, Inc.(NYC)
THAT'S NOT EXACTLY WHAT WE HAD IN MIND...
FORTUNATELY I ANTICIPATED YOUR REACTION.
PRESS "ONE" FOR SALES. PRESS "TWO" IN A HOPELESS EFFORT TO GET TECHNICAL SUPPORT.
2
S. Adams
PRESS "ONE" FOR ANSWERS TO QUESTIONS YOU DON'T HAVE. PRESS "TWO" IF YOU'RE GULLIBLE AND OPTIMISTIC.
2
9/20 © 1995 United Feature Syndicate, Inc.(NYC)
PRESS "TWO" IF YOU'RE WILLING TO BUY SOMETHING JUST SO YOU CAN TALK TO A HUMAN BEING...

I'VE BEEN ON HOLD FOR TECH SUPPORT SINCE TUESDAY. GET BOB AND MEET ME IN THE CAR.
I CAN'T WAIT TO TRY MY NEWEST MANEUVER, THE "TURBAN WEDGIE."
S. Adams
9/21 © 1995 United Feature Syndicate, Inc.(NYC)
IT STARTS LIKE A REGULAR WEDGIE THEN I WRAP IT AROUND HIS HEAD.
QUESTION...
ALICE, I'VE DECIDED TO ADD A RESOURCE TO YOUR PROJECT.
WE'RE HUMAN BEINGS, NOT "RESOURCES"!!
S. Adams
9/22 © 1995 United Feature Syndicate, Inc.(NYC)
WOULD IT HELP IF I TOLD YOU THAT RESOURCES ARE OUR MOST VALUABLE ASSET?

I FOUND SOFTWARE THAT HELPS MANAGERS WRITE PERFORMANCE EVALUATIONS!
UH-OH
IT'S MADE BY THE SAME COMPANY THAT MAKES FORTUNE COOKIES FOR CANADA!
THAT MAKES ME FEEL BETTER.
S. Adams
9/23 © 1995 United Feature Syndicate, Inc.(NYC)
NEXT DAY
"DON'T BUY A NEW CAR."
I DIDN'T THINK YOU KNEW HOW TO USE A PC.
MY SECRETARY WROTE THESE.

I HAVE TO TAKE A CONTRACT TO OUR COMPANY LAWYER. I NEED YOUR HELP, DOGBERT.
S. Adams
PLEASE REVIEW THIS CONTRACT. I NEED IT TODAY.
GIVE ME ALL OF YOUR COPIES PLUS THE ORIGINAL. THEN GO AWAY.
DON'T DO IT! HE PLANS TO LOSE THEM!!
GOOD DOG!
DANG!
I CANNOT APPROVE THIS. SOMEBODY MIGHT SUE US FOR NO GOOD REASON.
© 1995 United Feature Syndicate, Inc.(NYC)
9/24
THAT'S TRUE WITH ANY CONTRACT. ISN'T HE USING ABSURD LOGIC?
LET'S FIND OUT.
APPROVE THE CONTRACT NOW OR I'LL SUE YOU FOR OBSTRUCTION OF DOGS!!
OKAY OKAY
WOW
THE GREAT THING ABOUT ABSURD LOGIC IS THAT IT FITS ANY SITUATION.

WE'RE HAVING AN ISO 9000 AUDIT THIS WEEK.
TAKE A LOOK AT YOUR DOCUMENTED JOB DESCRIPTIONS AND MAKE SURE THAT IT'S WHAT YOU'RE DOING IF THE AUDITOR ASKS.
S. Adams
9/25 © 1995 United Feature Syndicate, Inc.(NYC)
ACCORDING TO THIS I'M SOME SORT OF ENGINEER.
AS IF WE'D HAVE TIME FOR THAT...
I'VE BEEN HIRED BY YOUR COMPANY TO PERFORM AN ISO 9000 AUDIT.
BASICALLY, YOU GIVE ME MONEY AND I TELL YOU THAT YOU'RE A BUNCH OF DOLTS. IT'S THE PERFECT JOB FOR ME.
S. Adams
9/26 © 1995 United Feature Syndicate, Inc.(NYC)
TELL ME WHAT YOU DO HERE, ALICE, IF THAT'S YOUR REAL NAME.
I'M AN ENGINEER. I MAKE SLIDES THAT PEOPLE CAN'T READ. SOMETIMES I EAT DONUTS.

HERE ARE THE RESULTS OF MY ISO 9000 AUDIT OF YOUR COMPANY.
YOUR EMPLOYEES ARE LARGELY UNTRAINED AND – I COULDN'T HELP NOTICE – FAIRLY UNATTRACTIVE.
S. Adams
9/27 © 1995 United Feature Syndicate, Inc.(NYC)
HOWEVER, THEY ARE ALSO HIGHLY SKILLED LIARS, SO YOU PASSED THE AUDIT EASILY.
WE SUCCEED WHERE IT COUNTS !!!

ALICE IS SITTING IN FOR THE BOSS!
S. Adams
PRODUCTIVITY AT LAST !!!
EFFICIENCY! YES!!
9/28 © 1995 United Feature Syndicate, Inc.(NYC)
AS LONG AS SHE DOESN'T GET AN ATTITUDE...

ALICE SITS IN FOR THE BOSS
I WILL APPROVE YOUR EXPENSE VOUCHER ON ONE CONDITION.
S. Adams
YOU MUST SLAY THE CREATURE WHO STALKS THE OFFICE AT NIGHT AND EATS OUR HIDDEN SNACKS!!!
9/29 © 1995 United Feature Syndicate, Inc.(NYC)
IT HAS TO BE EITHER YOU OR THE SECURITY GUARD.
SLAY HIM FIRST AND SEE IF THE PROBLEM STOPS.

YOU'RE MAKING A BIG MISTAKE. I'M NO ORDINARY MOUSE. IF YOU KISS ME I'LL TURN INTO A PRINCE!!!
S. Adams
DID I SAY "PRINCE"? I MEANT I'D BECOME THE SYMBOL FOR THE PERFORMER FORMERLY KNOWN AS PRINCE. HA HA HA!! GET IT?
9/30 © 1995 United Feature Syndicate, Inc.(NYC)
YOU'RE IMMUNE TO BOTH ROMANCE AND MIRTH. YOU MUST BE A... A...
THAT'S RIGHT. I'M AN ENGINEER.
TRASH

WISH ME LUCK, DOGBERT.
IF YOU GET MORE LUCK, WOULDN'T THERE BE LESS LUCK AVAILABLE FOR ME?
S. Adams
FOR "DESIRED SALARY" YOU WROTE "ONE MILLION DOLLARS."
YES, THANKS FOR ASKING.
PERHAPS THE QUESTION IS MISLEADING. THE APPLICATION SHOULD HAVE ASKED WHAT SALARY YOU EXPECT.
OH... WELL, I EXPECT YOU'LL HIRE SOMEBODY MORE QUALIFIED AND MY SALARY WILL REMAIN UNCHANGED.
© 1995 United Feature Syndicate, Inc.(NYC)
10-1
NO, TOO HONEST. I'M LOOKING FOR SOMETHING CLOSE TO REALITY, WITH MAYBE TWENTY-PERCENT FANTASY LAYERED ON TOP.
OKAY... I'D LIKE A FIFTEEN-PERCENT RAISE AND A LITTLE SHOULDER MASSAGE.
WHY DOES IT SEEM THAT I'M THE ONLY HONEST GUY ON EARTH?
YOUR TYPE TENDS NOT TO REPRODUCE.

WE'RE POISED FOR SUCCESS. WE EXPECT HUGE EARNINGS AND INCREASED MARKET SHARE!
NEXT ON THE AGENDA... THERE WILL BE NO RAISES BECAUSE IT WILL BE A DIFFICULT YEAR...
CAROL, I THOUGHT I TOLD YOU TO PUT THE "UNITED WAY" UPDATE BETWEEN THOSE TWO AGENDA ITEMS.
OOPSIE.
S. Adams
10/2 © 1995 United Feature Syndicate, Inc.(NYC)

YOUR RÉSUMÉ DOESN'T LIST ANY EXPERIENCE AS A JET PILOT, MISTER DOGBERT.
HOW HARD COULD IT BE?
YOU COULD SPEND A LOT OF MONEY ON SOME PRETTY BOY PILOT WITH EXPERIENCE, OR YOU CAN SAVE A FEW BUCKS AND HAVE ME DRIVE THE CORPORATE JET.
I AM UNDER A LOT OF BUDGET PRESSURE...AND I'M NOT ALLOWED ON THE JET MYSELF...
IT HAS A PILOT EJECT SEAT, RIGHT?
S. Adams
10/3 © 1995 United Feature Syndicate, Inc.(NYC)

DOGBERT, CORPORATE JET PILOT
ATTENTION, PASSENGER.
I'M CAPTAIN DOGBERT. THIS IS MY FIRST FLIGHT. I'LL BET YOU WISH YOU HADN'T CUT THE CORPORATE TRAINING BUDGET.
FOR SAFETY, KEEP AN EYE OUT THE WINDOW... IF IT LOOKS LIKE WE'RE GONNA HIT THE GROUND, TRY JUMPING UP RIGHT BEFORE IMPACT.
S. Adams
10/4 © 1995 United Feature Syndicate, Inc.(NYC)

DOGBERT, CORPORATE JET PILOT
THIS IS YOUR CAPTAIN SPEAKING...
IF YOU'D LIKE TO LAND SAFELY, THERE'S SOMETHING I'VE ALWAYS WANTED TO SEE A CEO DO.
THIS IS SO NOT FUNNY.
S. Adams
10/5 © 1995 United Feature Syndicate, Inc.(NYC)

THIS IS CAPTAIN DOGBERT WITH SOME GOOD NEWS AND SOME BAD NEWS.
THE GOOD NEWS IS THAT WE'LL BE HITTING TOWN TEN MINUTES AHEAD OF SCHEDULE...
THE BAD NEWS IS WE'LL BE HITTING TOWN.
S. Adams
10/6 © 1995 United Feature Syndicate, Inc.(NYC)

IT LOOKS LIKE THE PLANE'S GOING DOWN AND THERE'S ONLY ONE PARACHUTE.
GIVE IT TO ME!!! I'M A CEO WITH A HARVARD MBA. YOU'RE A DOG!!
THAT'S MY KNAPSACK.
OLD JOKE
S. Adams
10/7 © 1995 United Feature Syndicate, Inc.(NYC)

THAT'S FOUR HOURS THAT I'D LIKE TO HAVE BACK.
WHO CALLED THAT MEETING ANYWAY?
S. Adams
I MUST HAVE LEFT MY CALENDAR IN THERE.
OOOH
?
I'VE DISCOVERED A PRIMITIVE DONUT-SCAVENGING MAN CLAD ONLY IN YELLOW STICKY NOTES!!
I WAS ONCE LIKE YOU, BEFORE THE GREAT RIF.
© 1995 United Feature Syndicate, Inc.(NYC)
10-8
BUT RATHER THAN LEAVE IN HUMILIATION I DECIDED TO STAY AND LIVE OFF THE LAND LIKE OUR PROUD ANCESTORS.
TO ENSURE A BOUNTIFUL HARVEST I DO MY DONUT DANCE TO THE GODS.
WHEN THAT DOESN'T WORK I DISTRIBUTE MEETING NOTICES.
YOU'RE THE ONE!!

WE'LL SUCCEED IF WE UNDERSTAND WHO OUR COMPETITORS REALLY ARE!
MY COMPETITION IS DILBERT AND ALICE, WITH WHOM I COMPETE FOR SALARY INCREASES AND RARE PROMOTION OPPORTUNITIES.
I MEANT OUR EXTERNAL COMPETITION.
TELL ME AGAIN WHAT WE MAKE.
NO RAISE FOR YOU, IDIOT BOY.
S. Adams
10/9 © 1995 United Feature Syndicate, Inc.(NYC)
I'VE DECIDED TO GET MORE INVOLVED WITH YOUR PROJECT.
UH-OH.
UH-OH.
I'M JUST GOING TO ROLL UP MY SLEEVES AND PITCH IN.
DOES ANYBODY KNOW HOW TO WORK THESE BUTTONS?
S. Adams
10/10 © 1995 United Feature Syndicate, Inc.(NYC)

OKAY, JUST SHOW ME HOW TO PROGRAM SO I CAN HELP OUT ON YOUR PROJECT.
YOU'RE GOING TO BUILD A "G.U.I." USING OBJECT-ORIENTED DEVELOPMENT TOOLS...
G.U.I. IS PRONOUNCED "GOOEY."
I USED MY GUN OBJECT TO BLAST THE BUG OBJECT IN THE HALL OBJECT!!
NOTICE HOW GOOEY IT IS.
S. Adams
10/11 © 1995 United Feature Syndicate, Inc.(NYC)

OUR ORIGINAL PROJECT TIME LINE WAS TWELVE MONTHS... BUT SINCE YOU PITCHED IN TO HELP...
S. Adams
I DON'T HAVE AN EXACT END DATE, BUT IT'S ROUGHLY THE SAME TIME THAT THE SUN BECOMES A COLD DARK CHUNK OF COAL THE SIZE OF YOUR FOREHEAD.
10/12 © 1995 United Feature Syndicate, Inc.(NYC)
WE'LL NEED FLASH-LIGHTS.
AND SWEATERS. IT COULD GET NIPPY.

AS DIRECTOR OF HUMAN RESOURCES I HAVE DEVELOPED A POLICY FOR HANDLING THE EMPLOYEES WHO COMPLAIN.
S. Adams
IT'S A BIG HOLE. I'LL TRICK THE WHINERS INTO GETTING IN IT. AND THEN I'LL COVER THEM WITH SAND.
10/13 © 1995 United Feature Syndicate, Inc.(NYC)
I DON'T SEE HOW THIS COULD POSSIBLY WORK.
THERE'S A DETAILED EXPLANATION AT THE BOTTOM OF THE HOLE.
CATBERT THE H.R. DIRECTOR
MY JOB IS TOO STRESSFUL. CAN I SEE A COMPANY COUNSELOR?
S. Adams
I RE-ENGINEERED OUR COUNSELING PROCESS. NOW WE PUT YOU IN A BIG HOLE AND COVER YOU WITH SAND.
10/14 © 1995 United Feature Syndicate, Inc.(NYC)
IF THIS IS MY ONLY BENEFIT I'D BETTER GET A LOT OF SAND!
JUST KEEP YOUR MOUTH OPEN.

WHY DO YOU WANT TO BE OUR NEW "LONG RANGE PLANNER," MISTER DOGBERT?
BECAUSE "LONG RANGE" IS VERY FAR AWAY...
S. Adams
...THEREFORE IT WILL BE IMPOSSIBLE TO EVALUATE MY PERFORMANCE.
IF IT'S NOT TOO MUCH TO ASK, I'D LIKE TO BE ON FLEX-TIME SO YOU'LL NEVER KNOW IF I'M SUPPOSED TO BE AT WORK.
I'LL NEED AN INTERNFT LUNNECTION AT HOME SO I CAN TELECOMMUTE AND NOT POLLUTE.
BECAUSE I GIVE A HOOT.
© 1995 United Feature Syndicate, Inc.(NYC)
10-15
ALSO, I'D LIKE TO BE IN A GROUP WITH LOTS OF LOSERS. THAT WAY I'LL GET THE BIGGEST RAISE WHEN WE'RE RANKED.
YOU'RE HIRED. ALL OF THE OTHER APPLICANTS DEMANDED RELOCATION EXPENSES AND I HAVE NO BUDGET FOR THAT.
WHY DO I HAVE TO WORK WHILE YOU JUST LOOK FOR POODLE GRAPHICS ON THE INTERNET?
DON'T WORK TOO HARD; I'D LIKE A BIG RAISE.

I WONDER IF I'M WEARING ENOUGH FRAGRANCE.
S.Adams
AIEEEEEE!!
10/16 © 1995 United Feature Syndicate, Inc.(NYC)
I'D BETTER INCREASE THE DOSAGE UNTIL I HEAR SOME COMPLIMENTS.

DOGBERT, YOUR MISSION IS TO TELL MY CO-WORKER THAT HER PERFUME IS KILLING US. WEAR THIS GAS MASK.
S.Adams
USE HUMOR TO EASE THE TENSION.
GOOD IDEA.
10/17 © 1995 United Feature Syndicate, Inc.(NYC)
DID YOU HEAR THE JOKE ABOUT THE WOMAN WHO STANK LIKE A HOG RENDERING PLANT?
THREE TIMES TODAY...

I HAVE FAILED IN MY ATTEMPT TO SUBTLY TELL YOU THAT YOUR PERFUME IS KILLING PEOPLE. I WILL TRY A DIRECT APPROACH.
S.Adams
HEY!! YOU SMELL BAD!!!
B-A-A-A-D!!
10/18 © 1995 United Feature Syndicate, Inc.(NYC)
SHOULD I GIVE YOU CPR?
NO-O-O-O!! LET ME DIE!!

WELCOME TO HEAVEN, MISTER DOGBERT.
WOW, IT LOOKS LIKE YOU GUYS RELAXED YOUR STANDARDS!
S. Adams
DOGS ARE AUTOMATIC. NO MATTER WHAT YOU DO, THERE'S ALWAYS A PLACE IN HEAVEN FOR EVERY LITTLE DOG.
10/19 © 1995 United Feature Syndicate, Inc.(NYC)
I'D LIKE THAT BACK NOW, IF YOU DON'T MIND!!
WHAT KIND OF DISTANCE CAN YOU GET WITH THESE LITTLE "FRISBEES"?

MISTER DOGBERT, WE'VE DECIDED TO SEND YOU BACK TO EARTH AS AN ANGEL.
S. Adams
YOUR MISSION IS TO HELP PEOPLE IN NEED. WE HAVE GIVEN YOU SPECIAL POWERS.
WE'LL BE WATCHING.
10/20 © 1995 United Feature Syndicate, Inc.(NYC)
OKAY, SO WHAT'S THE PRICE FOR NEW HAIR PLUS BUNS OF STEEL?
AHEM
IT'S ALL ON THE PRICE SHEET.

ARE YOU SAYING THAT YOU'RE AN ANGEL NOW? AND YOU HAVE SPECIAL POWERS TO HELP PEOPLE.
S. Adams
EXACTLY. I INSTINCTIVELY KNOW WHAT PEOPLE WANT AND I CAN GIVE IT TO THEM WITH A SNAP OF THE PAW.
SNAP
10/21 © 1995 United Feature Syndicate, Inc.(NYC)
ARE YOU HAVING ANY TROUBLE CONTROLLING IT?
MY AIM STINKS.

THIS GRAPHIC SHOWS OUR BIGGEST OBSTACLE TO SUCCESS.
S. Adams
RDS ZPL ABP
NDP QRT LNP
?
?
?
ARE YOU SAYING OUR BIGGEST OBSTACLE TO SUCCESS IS POOR GRAPHICS?
I THINK HE'S SAYING OUR BIGGEST PROBLEM IS HIS OVERALL INABILITY TO COMMUNICATE.
© 1995 United Feature Syndicate, Inc.(NYC)
10/22
I THINK HIS POINT GOES BEYOND COMMUNICATION. HE'S SHOWING US THAT HE DOESN'T EVEN THINK CLEARLY!
THAT'S IT!
HIGH FIVE!!
YOU BROKE THE CODE!
YOU KNOW HOW I SAID YOU SHOULD PARTICIPATE MORE IN MEETINGS?
I DIDN'T MEAN IT.

WE'VE DECIDED TO REVOKE YOUR ANGEL STATUS. YOU'RE GIVING US ALL A BAD NAME.
YOUR PROBLEM IS THAT YOU DEFINE "HEALING" TOO NARROWLY. I'M MAKING UGLY PEOPLE LOOK ATTRACTIVE, AND THAT'S IMPORTANT, TOO.
IS IT TOO LATE TO GO BACK TO MY OLD LOOK?
WHY? YOU'RE BEAUTIFUL!
S. Adams
10/23 © 1995 United Feature Syndicate, Inc.(NYC)

CAROL, ABOUT THIS FLIGHT TO NEW YORK THAT YOU BOOKED FOR ME...
IS IT REALLY NECESSARY TO MAKE ALL THESE STOPOVERS IN THIRD-WORLD COUNTRIES THAT ARE EXPERIENCING REBEL INSURRECTIONS?
YOU'D BETTER WEAR THE INTERNATIONAL SYMBOL OF THE "RED CROSS" ON YOUR BACK.
S. Adams
10/24 © 1995 United Feature Syndicate, Inc.(NYC)

TERRIBLE NEWS: MY BOSS ASSIGNED ME TO A FUN AND VALUABLE PROJECT.
UH-OH. THAT MEANS AT LEAST THREE MORONS WILL BE ASSIGNED TO SIMILAR PROJECTS. YOU MUST FIND THEM AND CRUSH THEM...
EXACTLY.
CARL, OLD BUDDY, WHATCHA WORKIN' ON THESE DAYS?
NOTHING FUN AND VALUABLE. SHOO SHOO!!
S. Adams
10/25 © 1995 United Feature Syndicate, Inc.(NYC)

WALLY AND I HAVE A BET ABOUT WHY YOU ASSIGNED ME TO THE SAME TASK AS THREE OTHER PEOPLE.
S. Adams
I BELIEVE IT'S A CLEVER PLOY TO CREATE HEALTHY INTERNAL COMPETITION. WALLY THINKS YOU'RE JUST DUMBER THAN THE AVERAGE CAULIFLOWER.
10/26 © 1995 United Feature Syndicate, Inc.(NYC)
MAY I POINT OUT THAT CAULIFLOWER IS THE BRAIN OF THE FRUIT KINGDOM.
YES!

THREE OTHER PEOPLE ASKED FOR THAT SAME INFORMATION. YOU MUST BE ON REDUNDANT PROJECTS.
S. Adams
HERE'S A BIG BINDER WHICH AT FIRST GLANCE SEEMS USEFUL, BUT YOU'LL REALIZE LATER IT'S NOT.
10/27 © 1995 United Feature Syndicate, Inc.(NYC)
I'VE GOT A FEW MORE USELESS BINDERS. DO YOU WANT 'EM?
SURE. I'M USING THEM TO BUILD AN ADDITION TO MY CUBICLE.

IT LOOKS LIKE SOMEBODY IS USING BINDERS TO ILLEGALLY INCREASE THE SIZE OF HIS CUBICLE.
S. Adams
YOU THINK YOUR STATUS WILL INCREASE WITH YOUR CUBICLE SIZE, DON'T YOU! WELL, IT WON'T WORK!
10/28 © 1995 United Feature Syndicate, Inc.(NYC)
HERE'S A RAISE. I DON'T KNOW WHY.
PSSST. IS HE SEEING ANYBODY?
RRRR

HELEN, DO YOU HAVE ANY STAPLES IN THE SUPPLY CABINET?
NO, I ONLY STOCK THE BASICS: CHEAP PENS WITH GREEN INK, BIG JARS OF GLUE AND RIBBONS FOR OBSOLETE PRINTERS.
S. Adams
COULD YOU ORDER SOME STAPLES?
YOU NEED TO GIVE ME THE ORDER NUMBER.
OKAY. CAN I SEE YOUR SUPPLY CATALOG?
WALLY BORROWED IT.
I'D BETTER GET THAT; IT MIGHT BE PERSONAL.
SOB
RRRING
© 1995 United Feature Syndicate, Inc.(NYC)
10/29
WALLY, DO YOU HAVE THE...
I NEED YOUR HELP WITH THIS. PULL UP A CHAIR.
I NEED BOTH OF YOU TO COME TALK TO A VENDOR THAT WE'LL NEVER USE.
THANKS TO TEAMWORK, I ALMOST STAPLED SOMETHING TODAY.
I'M SO PROUD TO KNOW YOU.

HEADQUARTERS
HEY, CHUCK'S LOOKING UNHAPPY TODAY. WHAT'S THE PROBLEM, BIG GUY?
S. Adams
ALL OF MY BAD DECISIONS ARE CATCHING UP TO ME. COULD WE DO ANOTHER REORG TO COVER MY TRACKS?
YEAH, I'VE GOT SOME BODIES TO BURY, TOO.
10/30 © 1995 United Feature Syndicate, Inc.(NYC)
"...THESE CHANGES WILL ALLOW US TO FOCUS ON OUR CORE BUSINESS."
WHOA! LET ME GET MY REORG BOOTS.

I DON'T UNDERSTAND HOW THE NEW REORGANIZATION WILL HELP US "FOCUS ON OUR CORE BUSINESS."
S. Adams
DID OUR CORE BUSINESS CHANGE? OR ARE YOU SAYING THAT EVERY REORG PRIOR TO THIS WAS A MISDIRECTED FAILURE?
10/31 © 1995 United Feature Syndicate, Inc.(NYC)
WALLY, WHEN A CAR GETS A FLAT TIRE, WHAT DO YOU DO?
WELL, IF I'M YOU, I ROTATE THE TIRES AND DRIVE HOME.

GUESS WHAT, WALLY.
WHAT SADISTIC PLOT HAS H.R. COME UP WITH NOW, CATBERT?
S. Adams
WE'RE GIVING YOU A REAL BOSS PLUS A "DOTTED LINE" TO ANOTHER BOSS WHO HAS DIFFERENT OBJECTIVES.
11/1 © 1995 United Feature Syndicate, Inc.(NYC)
THE STATUS REPORTS ALONE WILL TAKE FORTY HOURS A WEEK.
I'M GONNA STAPLE MYSELF TO DEATH.

I HEARD YOU GOT ASSIGNED ON A "DOTTED LINE" TO OUR BOSS' ARCH-RIVAL.
GROAN
S. Adams
LOOK ON THE BRIGHT SIDE. THINK OF YOURSELF AS LEADING THE EXCITING LIFE OF A SECRET DOUBLE-AGENT!
11/2 © 1995 United Feature Syndicate, Inc.(NYC)
DON'T MOST DOUBLE-AGENTS GET CAPTURED AND EXECUTED IMMEDIATELY?
THEY WISH IT WAS IMMEDIATE.

THE "DOGBERT CORPORATE ART SOURCE" WILL PROVIDE LOW-COST PAINTINGS FOR YOUR WALLS.
S. Adams
OUR MOTTO IS "IF IT'S IN A FRAME IT WILL LOOK LIKE ART TO YOU."
11/3 © 1995 United Feature Syndicate, Inc.(NYC)
HOW MUCH DO THE PAINTINGS COST?
SIX DOLLARS A POUND.

HOW DID YOU GET THE CONTRACT TO SUPPLY OUR COMPANY WITH WALL ART?
LOW BID.
S. Adams
AS WE SPEAK, MY ASSISTANT IS SCOURING THE EARTH IN SEARCH OF LOW-COST ART.
11/4 © 1995 United Feature Syndicate, Inc.(NYC)
SCHOOL-o-ART
I'LL TAKE IT!!

I WORKED ALL NIGHT BUT I FINISHED THE PRESENTATION PACKAGE YOU WANTED.
PUT THE PRESENTATION DATE ON EACH PAGE.
S. Adams
THOSE ARE COLOR TRANSPARENCIES. IT WOULD TAKE HOURS AND COST HUNDREDS OF DOLLARS TO REPRINT THEM.
THERE'S NO REASON TO DATE THEM. IN FACT, IT WOULD LIMIT FUTURE USE AND CLUTTER THE PAGE.
BUT SINCE YOU'RE INCAPABLE OF ADMITTING ERROR...
© 1995 United Feature Syndicate, Inc.(NYC)
11/5
I EAGERLY AWAIT YOUR BIZARRE, OTHER-WORLDLY EXPLANATION FOR PUTTING THE DATE ON EACH PAGE.
SOME PEOPLE MIGHT NOT HAVE CALENDARS. AND WE HAVE TO MAKE SURE IT'S NOT A HOLIDAY.
BAM!
OUCH. MY BRAIN EXPLODED.
THE FIRST PRESENTATION IS FEBRUARY 30TH...

I'VE COME TO BE YOUR PERSONAL DIGITAL ASSISTANT.
USE THE LITTLE PEN TO WRITE MESSAGES ON MY STOMACH. I'LL USE STATE-OF-THE-RAT TECHNOLOGY TO INTERPRET YOUR HANDWRITING.
WEAVE... ME... A... CONE... YOO... CUPID... BAT...
S. Adams
11/6 © 1995 United Feature Syndicate, Inc.(NYC)
WHY ARE YOU PUTTING A SIGN ON THE COFFEE MAKER?
COFFEE MAKER
IT'S AN ISO 9000 REQUIREMENT. EVERY-THING MUST BE CLEARLY LABELED. THERE CAN BE NO EXCEPTIONS.
THAT'S STUPID.
BELIEVE ME, I DON'T LIKE IT ANY MORE THAN YOU DO.
STUPID LABEL GUY
S. Adams
11/7 © 1995 United Feature Syndicate, Inc.(NYC)

THE PROJECT STATUS IS "YELLOW LIGHT."
IN USER TESTS WE FOUND THAT THE PRODUCT LOCKS UP EVERY TWELVE SECONDS. THE INTERFACE IS INCOM-PREHENSIBLE AND THE MANUAL IS PURE FICTION.
I THINK IT'S CLEAR WHAT WE NEED TO DO...
SHIP IT AND HOPE SOMEBODY WRITES A "DUMMIES" BOOK ABOUT IT?
S. Adams
11/8 © 1995 United Feature Syndicate, Inc.(NYC)

SAINT DOGBERT ENTERS THE LAND OF CUBICLES SEARCHING FOR THE DEMONS OF STUPIDITY.
S. Adams
SUDDENLY HE FINDS AN OVER-PROMOTED COMPUTER GURU SPOUTING USELESS DATABASE CONCEPTS.
YOU'D BE FOOLS TO IGNORE THE BOOLEAN ANTI-BINARY LEAST-SQUARE APPROACH.
11/9 © 1995 United Feature Syndicate, Inc.(NYC)
THE MONSTER IS DISPATCHED TO THE DARK WORLD BY THE SIGHT OF ITS MOST FEARED OBJECT.
LOOK! ACTUAL CODE!
COOL!
SSSS SSS

HOW LONG WILL IT TAKE TO FIX ANY PROBLEMS WE FIND IN OUR BETA PRODUCT?
S. Adams
IT IS LOGICALLY IMPOSSIBLE TO SCHEDULE FOR THE UNKNOWN.
11/10 © 1995 United Feature Syndicate, Inc.(NYC)
TRY TO THINK AS A MANAGER, NOT AS AN ENGINEER.
IN THAT CASE, WE'LL FIX THE PROBLEMS BEFORE WE FIND THEM.

THIS NEXT TRANSPARENCY IS AN INCOMPREHENSIBLE JUMBLE OF COMPLEXITY AND UNDEFINED ACRONYMS.
S. Adams
YOU MIGHT WONDER WHY I'M GOING TO SHOW IT TO YOU SINCE THE ONLY POSSIBLE RESULT IS TO LOWER YOUR OPINION OF MY COMMUNICATION SKILLS.
11/11 © 1995 United Feature Syndicate, Inc.(NYC)
FRANKLY, IT'S BECAUSE I LIKE MAKING COMPLEX PICTURES MORE THAN I LIKE YOU.

MISTER CATBERT WILL EXPLAIN OUR NEW "TOTAL COMPENSATION PLAN" FOR EXCELLENCE.
S. Adams
WE NO LONGER VIEW COMPENSATION IN THE NARROW TERMS OF SALARY ALONE.
DANGER! DANGER!
IF EMPLOYEE BENEFITS GO UP, THEN SALARIES CAN GO DOWN AND IT ALL BALANCES OUT.
FOR EXAMPLE, DID YOU KNOW YOU COULD LOWER YOUR BLOOD PRESSURE BY RUBBING MY SOFT, FURRY BELLY?
© 1995 United Feature Syndicate, Inc.(NYC)
11/12
IT MIGHT BE A TRICK!
WHAT'S THE WORST THING THAT COULD HAPPEN?
HA HA HA!!! IT'S A HEALTH BENEFIT! NOW I'LL CUT EVERYBODY'S SALARY!
I'VE NOTICED THAT THE MORE HEALTH BENEFITS I GET, THE WORSE I FEEL.

OUR GOAL IS TO WRITE BUG-FREE SOFTWARE. I'LL PAY A TEN-DOLLAR BONUS FOR EVERY BUG YOU FIND AND FIX.
S. Adams
YAHOO!
WE'RE RICH
YES!!! YES!!! YES!!!
11/13 © 1995 United Feature Syndicate, Inc.(NYC)
I HOPE THIS DRIVES THE RIGHT BEHAVIOR.
I'M GONNA WRITE ME A NEW MINIVAN THIS AFTERNOON!

THE COMPANY PAYS ME TEN DOLLARS FOR EVERY BUG I FIX IN MY CODE, RATBERT.
S. Adams
I WANT YOU TO DO YOUR LITTLE RAT DANCE ON MY KEYBOARD SO I'LL HAVE LOTS OF BUGS TO FIX.
11/14 © 1995 United Feature Syndicate, Inc.(NYC)
HOW AM I DOING?
NOT SO GOOD. YOU JUST AUTHORED A WEB BROWSER.

MY ACCOMPLISHMENT THIS WEEK IS THAT I'VE BECOME AN AGENT OF CHANGE.
S. Adams
I FOSTER AND REWARD THOSE BEHAVIORS THAT CONTRIBUTE TO A CULTURE OF TEAMWORK.
11/15 © 1995 United Feature Syndicate, Inc.(NYC)
I'VE BECOME SLIGHTLY MORE CYNICAL.
KEEP UP THE GOOD WORK, BUDDY.
PAT PAT

I USED TO WRITE PROGRAMS USING PUNCH CARDS... BUT I'D RATHER BE FISHING...
LOOK, YOU BEARDED ROAD APPLE, IF YOU ANSWER ONE MORE OF MY QUESTIONS WITH AN IRRELEVANT STORY I'LL SNAP YOU INTO NEXT WEEK!!
S. Adams
11/16 © 1995 United Feature Syndicate, Inc.(NYC)
SOMETIME NEXT WEEK...
LOOKS LIKE A HOLE IN THE SPACE-TIME CONTINUUM.
DID YOU HEAR A SNAP?
I THINK WE SHOULD BUILD AN SQL DATABASE.
UH-OH
DOES HE UNDERSTAND WHAT HE SAID OR IS IT SOMETHING HE SAW IN A TRADE MAGAZINE AD?
S. Adams
11/17 © 1995 United Feature Syndicate, Inc.(NYC)
WHAT COLOR DO YOU WANT THAT DATABASE?
I THINK MAUVE HAS THE MOST RAM.

FROM NOW ON I'M GOING TO BE MORE PROACTIVE.
YOU'RE FIRED!!
S. Adams
11/18 © 1995 United Feature Syndicate, Inc.(NYC)
FOR WHAT??
I DON'T KNOW YET. THAT'S THE PROBLEM WITH BEING PROACTIVE.

WE NEED TO SHIP THE V-1 PRODUCT TOMORROW. I PROMISED OUR CEO HE CAN ANNOUNCE IT AT THE SHAREHOLDER MEETING.
S. Adams
THAT'S TWO MONTHS EARLY!!
WE HAVEN'T ADDED ANY FEATURES YET!!
WHAT WOULD WE SHIP? OUR LAB PROTOTYPE IS THE ONLY V-1 IN EXISTENCE!
NO...YOU WOULDN'T!
I'VE SCHEDULED PRESS TOURS SO YOU CAN DO DEMOS ALL NEXT WEEK.
ON WHAT?!
WE'LL NEED TWENTY THOUSAND DOLLARS TO BUILD ANOTHER PROTOTYPE!
© 1995 United Feature Syndicate, Inc.(NYC)
THAT REMINDS ME; I FROZE THE BUDGET FOR THE REST OF THE YEAR.
11/19
IF THERE'S ANYTHING YOU'D LIKE ME TO DO, DON'T HESITATE TO ASK.
YEAH, I'D LIKE YOU TO DO SOME-THING...
OOH... I THINK I SHOULD HAVE HESITATED TO ASK THAT.